SHERYL LINDSELL-ROBERTS

135 Tips
for
Writing
Successful
Business
Documents

Houghton Mifflin Company
Boston ▪ New York

Visit our website: **www.houghtonmifflinbooks.com**

Library of Congress Cataloging-in-Publication Data

Lindsell-Roberts, Sheryl.
  135 tips for writing successful business documents / Sheryl Lindsell-Roberts
Houghton Mifflin Company.-- 1st ed.
          p. cm.
  ISBN-13: 978-0-618-65991-3
  ISBN-10: 0-618-65991-9
  1. Business writing--Handbooks, manuals, etc. 2. Commercial correspondence--Handbooks, manuals, etc. I. Title: One hundred thirty five tips for writing successful business documents. II. Title.
  HF5726.L57 2006
  651.7'4--dc22

                                                            2005033828

Manufactured in the United States of America

Book design by Catherine Hawkes, Cat & Mouse

QUM 10 9 8 7 6 5 4 3 2 1

Author photograph courtesy of Turner Photography, Malden, MA.

Sample mission statements on pages 115–116 courtesy of Baystate Connections and KidsWin. PowerPoint is a registered trademark of Microsoft Corporation.

To Harry Lorenz, the world's greatest brother.

On the surface we may not appear to be much alike. But deep down, we are. As children, we lived and fought together. We laughed and cried together. We shared our dreams and our plans. As adults, we share the same history, the same values, the same sorrows, and the same family stories that are tucked away in our memories. It's a bond no other people share. It's hard to imagine what my life would be like without having Harry as my loving brother and very special friend.

CONTENTS

MESSAGE 13

DRAFTING 18

VISUAL IMPACT 21

TONE 30

PROOFREADING AND EDITING 43

PART TWO

Moving Forward: A Wide Array of Business Documents 47

ABSTRACTS 49

ARTICLES 51

BROCHURES 56

BUSINESS PLANS 63

COLLABORATIVE WRITING 68

ACKNOWLEDGMENTS

I want to express my heartfelt thanks to my family (blood and extended) and my dear friends. Without their love and support, I wouldn't be the person I am today and wouldn't be living my dreams.

I want especially to thank Marge Berube, Vice President, Publisher of Dictionaries, at Houghton Mifflin, who asked me to write this book and shows continued confidence in me. I also want to thank Catherine Pratt, Editor, who made sure my *i*'s were dotted, my *t*'s were crossed, and much more.

INTRODUCTION

I read things that are absolutely incomprehensible. . . . I shudder
to think how Thomas Jefferson's Declaration of Independence
would have read in standard, government-worker bureaucrat-
speak. It would be ten times as long, one-tenth as comprehensive,
and would have lacked all inspiration.

BOB KERREY
former US senator and governor of Nebraska

The National Center on the Evaluation of Quality in the Workplace conducted a study in which they asked American employers to identify the skills they considered most important to job performance. The employers listed communication as the second most critical job skill. (Attitude was number one.)

Employers equate communication skills with the ability to think clearly, examine alternatives, analyze information, and make decisions. Everything you write must hit the mark because your career depends on it. As a skilled business writer you

- Influence decisions and provide leadership
- Inspire action and get results
- Generate business and maintain goodwill
- Land a job and advance in your career
- Save money and manage time efficiently.

Poor Writing Costs Millions of Dollars

In his July 4, 2005 article "Poor Writing Costs Taxpayers Millions," Justin Pope, AP education writer, reports that according to a new study, states spend $221 million annually on remedial writing training. The study, completed by the National Commission on Writing, says that poor writing and unclear instructions are slowing down government employees and resulting in soaring costs for taxpayers.

Arkansas governor Mike Huckabee, vice chairman of the National Governors Association which conducted the survey for the commission, stated, "It's impossible to calculate the ultimate cost of lost productivity because people have to read [and write] things two and three times." Another cost, he said, is the loss of good ideas. "There are some really bright people who can't communicate and as a result their ideas probably aren't given the attention they deserve."

There Will Always Be Power in the Written Word

Technology hasn't replaced the need to write clearly and concisely; it's merely simplified the process. Whether you use a hammer and chisel, a tired old computer, or state-of-the-art technology, the written word is the end result—the document by which you're judged. For example, how many times have you received e-mail messages that have spelling errors, poor grammar, no capitalization, or worse? Probably too many times to count. How do you judge the sender? Think of the way you want to be judged and the way you want to be remembered.

Why I Wrote This Book

I wrote this book to share with you the outgrowth of more than twenty years of successful business writing experience (and perhaps to make enough money to retire in style)! Part of my experience comes from facilitating a variety of business and technical writing workshops in the business, academic, and government arenas. And part of my experience comes from the strategic business writing and marketing campaigns I generate for my clients. All this experience is rolled into these pages, together with highlights from my nineteen other books.

How to Read This Book

Part One is the section to read sequentially. It walks you through the basics for writing all business documents: understanding your audience, purpose, and key issue; generating headlines; writing the draft; designing for visual impact; honing the tone; and proofreading. Part Two focuses on specific types of business documents. In this part, jump to whatever topic interests you or applies to your writing challenge. You will see several icons as you go through this book. Here's what they mean:

 Hot tip. This may be a time saver, life saver, frustration saver, or just about anything relevant to the issue at hand.

Reminder. This is a virtual string to tie around your finger so you won't forget something important, such as packing your umbrella during monsoon season.

Word from Sheryl. This is an opportunity to share "war stories" that my clients find helpful when I present workshops. It also shares stories my clients have told me. They include the blissful, the painful, and everything in between.

A Word About Gender

I searched for a pronoun to cover both genders. Unfortunately, I wasn't able to find one, and it isn't always appropriate to make a sentence plural. Rather than getting into the clumsy *he/she* or *him/her* pronouns,

I opted to be an equal opportunity writer. I tossed a coin, and here's how it landed: I use the male gender in the even tips and the female gender in the odd tips. (If this offends anyone, I apologize.)

Sheryl Lindsell-Roberts, M.A.

P.S. Keep this book for easy reference. Don't share it. You may never get it back!

Getting Started

D o the documents you write help you to close new business? Do they shout *Read me*? Do they get the attention they deserve? Do they drive the action you want or expect?

If you answer no to even one of these questions, Part One can make the difference. Many people—even the brightest and most capable—aren't satisfied with their business writing and would rather have root-canal surgery than commit something to the (dreaded) written word, so you're not alone. The good news is that great writing isn't wired into DNA. Everyone (no matter how anxious) can learn to write clearly, strategically, and persuasively. And your writing can be directly responsible for bringing in new business or propelling your career.

Part One takes you through a process that has helped thousands of businesspeople to write with confidence and competence.

Go through this process before you begin any writing, and you too will write with confidence and competence.

It's critical that you plan your document before you begin to write it. Just as with any project, when you plan you have better results. Tips 1 through 13 take you through the planning process of getting started, writing headlines, and sequencing.

Once you start using this process, planning won't take you more than just a few minutes, and you'll be amazed at the results. Workshop participants typically tell me that when they plan properly using the steps in Part One, they cut writing time by 30 to 50 percent and get the results they want.

*Your audience is one single reader. I have found that
sometimes it helps to pick out one person—a real person
you know, or an imagined person—and write to that one.*

JOHN STEINBECK

Everyone suffers from writer's block at some time. You sit and stare at a blank piece of paper or computer screen and hope something materializes. When you understand your reader, you're prepared to write strategically and persuasively—affecting your reader as you wish. Even Mark Twain, a prolific writer, had trouble getting started. He'd leave a sentence unfinished, so that when he sat down for his next writing session there would be an easy kickoff point.

Following is a Start Up Sheet that walks you through the process of determining critical elements for strategic writing. This is the first step to cutting writing time by 30 to 50 percent and getting the results you want. After the first time, filling out the Start Up Sheet will take you only a few minutes. You'll wonder how you ever wrote without it.

Identify your primary reader. Do you have multiple readers?

If you want to hit your target, you must know exactly where to aim. Identify your reader and your relationship (if any).

- Is your reader a manager, peer, subordinate, client, customer?
- Is your reader technical or nontechnical?
- What does your reader look like?
- What color hair does she have?
- What color are her shoes?

START UP SHEET

Reader

1. Who is my primary reader? Do I have multiple levels of readers?

2. What does my reader *need to know* about the topic?

3. What's in it for my reader?

4. Does my writing need a special angle or point of view?

5. What's my reader's attitude toward the topic?

Purpose

6. My purpose is to _____, so my reader will _____.

Key Issue

7. What's the one key point I want my reader to remember?

Yes, this sounds very basic. But think about it. It's easy to write to a reader you know, because you know her. Even when you don't know your reader personally, you must attempt to know her. Try to make her real, even if you have to invent her. Imagine her as a person, rather than a faceless humanoid.

> I recently wrote an annual report for a company and pretended I was writing it for my brother. Although my brother is highly intelligent, he's unfamiliar with the industry. My goal was simply to give him the information I would have wanted him to give me if our positions had been reversed. If you have no siblings, it's okay to borrow my brother. His name is Harry.

When you write to multiple readers, rank them in their order of importance or on the basis of who will take action. If you're writing a long message to multiple readers, consider meeting the needs of each audience in clearly identified sections of your document. For example, address the needs of top managers in an executive summary, the needs of people who want details in the body, and the needs of technical specialists in an appendix.

2 Understand what your reader *needs to know* about the subject.

The focus is on *needs to know*. Too often we tell readers everything we can about a topic. Think of what your reader needs to know, not what he already knows. You don't want to give too much or too little information. Consider these questions:

- What's the reader's level of knowledge about the subject?
- Does he have any preconceived notions?
- Are there barriers to his understanding your message?
- What acronyms, initialisms, or abbreviations will he need explained?

People with academic, scientific, or technical backgrounds tend to be process-oriented. They benefit from step-by-step explanations. Those with backgrounds in business or law are answer-oriented. They respond to quick answers. Creative people are usually visually oriented and benefit from charts, tables, and other visual representations.

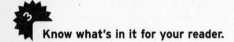

Know what's in it for your reader.

When you receive a message, you mentally ask yourself, What's in it for me? Why is this worth my time? Your reader will ask those same questions. Maybe what's in it for her is an opportunity to make her job easier, to look good to her superiors, to be more knowledgeable, or to propel her career path. Make clear what's in it for your reader.

I was preparing a marketing program for a large software company. I met with the technical managers, and they handed me a tome of bits and bytes and nuts and bolts. I could have taken that information and written something very professional and very technical. However, that wasn't going to sell their product. This company sells software for $100,000 and up; therefore, a salesperson's initial contact would be with a CEO, CIO, or some C-level person. C-level people don't spend money on technology; they spend money on *solutions to business problems*.

In order to help the technical managers understand what we needed to include, I took them through a process of "So what?" With the answer to each "So what?" we moved closer to the bottom-line benefits. We determined that the software would gauge the success of marketing campaigns, analyze trends, and measure customer satisfaction. Such benefits are normally intangibles. Articulating them can give a big boost to a company's bottom line.

Determine if your writing needs a special angle or point of view.

You determine the point of view by understanding the needs of your reader. Managers, for example, are big-picture people. They need the key issue. Technical people need the details. Salespeople need the benefits.

Anticipate your reader's attitude toward the subject.

You may not always tell your reader what she wants to hear, but you must tell her what she needs to know. Will she be *responsive* or *glad to get your message*? Will she be *neutral*? Will she be *unresponsive* or *disappointed*? Consider these questions:

- Are you disputing existing data?
- Will your reader lose face by accepting your recommendation?
- Will your message create more work for her?
- Will your reader get pressure from her manager because of your message?
- Do you want to fire the reader's son?

Pinpoint your purpose and action item.

My purpose is to _____, so my reader will
_____.

Let's break this into two parts:

1. My purpose is to _____, . . .

Whether you think your purpose is to communicate, to inform, to sell, to teach, or whatever, chances are you're trying to *persuade* someone to do something. The following are persuasive and generic purposes:

Persuasive: You're trying to *persuade* your reader to make a purchase.
Generic: You're writing to *inform* your reader of a new product offering.

Persuasive: You're trying to *persuade* your manager that your ideas are worth listening to.
Generic: You want to *tell* your manager an idea you have that could save the company money.

When you realize that 99 percent of all the business writing you do is to persuade someone to do something, you start to write strategically, rather than generically.

2. . . . so my reader will _____.

When your reader knows exactly what action you want him to take, he can digest your message more intelligently. Do you want him to turn the case over to the legal department? Discontinue testing? Call the bank? Refund the money? Halt shipping? Take this up with his manager? Wait to hear from you? Write a new contract? Pass the message to someone else? Send a check? Make a purchase? Do nothing?

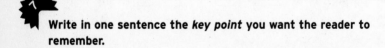

Write in one sentence the *key point* you want the reader to remember.

Billboard advertisers, ad people, and designers know that people read on the fly. Kids know this too. Have you ever found (or left) a note on the table saying, "Don't forget to leave me $5—I'll explain later"?

Business readers want the key issue so they can get to the point immediately. Put on your advertising hat. Pretend you have to write a 15-second commercial. If your reader forgets everything else, what's the one point you want her to remember? Condense this key point into one sentence.

You don't write because you want to say something;
you write because you have something to say.

F. SCOTT FITZGERALD, *The Crack-Up*

Delivery involves knowing who should receive a copy of the message, the best way to deliver the message, and the best time to send the message.

Know who should receive a copy of the message.

Are you copying people because they need to see the document or is this for CYA (cover your anatomy) purposes? Send messages only to people who need to receive them. You don't get points for adding to people's information overload.

> In an e-mail environment it is especially important to consider who is on your distribution list. People have a tendency to press the Send button and copy the immediate world. With everyone suffering from information overload, be considerate. Send messages only to people who need to receive them, just as you would with paper-based mail.
>
> If you send only the information people need to do their jobs well and don't contribute to their overload, they'll approach anything they receive from you with respect.

Understand the best way to deliver the message.

What's the best method of delivery? Paper? E-mail? Fax? Phone? In person? Meeting? Federal Express? Pony express?

I scheduled a meeting with a Boston-based client for 8:00 one morning. I called the day before to confirm the date and time. When I arrived at the client's office the morning of the meeting, she looked puzzled. "What are you doing here?" she asked. "Didn't we have a meeting scheduled for this morning?" I answered. "Didn't you get my message?" she questioned.

Here's what happened: My client worked late the evening before trying to prepare for our meeting. Realizing she wouldn't be ready, she sent me an e-mail at 8:30 p.m. telling me that we needed to reschedule. I have a life, and I don't read e-mails at 8:30 in the evening. Had she called, I would have known not to show up. This is a classic case of someone sending an e-mail without thinking of the best way to deliver the message to the reader. She should have phoned me.

With the advent of modern technology, we can embarrass ourselves in a number of ways. Think before you send. When selecting a delivery method, consider these guidelines:

Delivery	Best Used for
Letter	Initial contacts or formal communications.
E-mail	Quick, informal messaging.
Memo	Internal communications you want to circulate and perhaps post on a bulletin board.
Fax	Sending drawings, contracts, or anything that needs to be delivered in its original form. Gets signatures in record time.
Phone call	Scheduling appointments, delivering information quickly, or sharing give-and-take conversations. (Conference calls are a good way to involve several people in a conversation.)

In person	Providing initial meetings when you want to develop long-term relationships.
Videoconference	Replacing travel when you need to get people face to face.

10 Know the best time to deliver the message.

Timing is everything. When is it too early? When is it too late? For example, if it's noon and you need to let people know about a 1:00 meeting, an e-mail message may not do. Phone the people and/or leave notes on their computer screens.

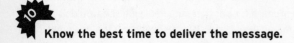 A participant in one of my workshops worked for a major university. In mid-May she sent out a letter to incoming freshmen informing them of check-in procedures, parking policies, and more for the fall term. In August she was barraged with phone calls inquiring about these issues, and she didn't know why.

It's because the timing of her letter was way off. Students who haven't yet graduated from high school and have a whole summer ahead of them aren't thinking about check-in procedures and parking policies. If she mails the letters closer to the time students need the information, they will pay attention. Timing *is* everything!

> *The difficulty . . . is not to write, but to write*
> *what you mean; not to affect your reader, but to*
> *affect him precisely as you wish.*

ROBERT LOUIS STEVENSON

Once you fill out the Start Up Sheet and understand delivery issues, it's time to get more specific about the message. This is still part of the planning process. As a writer, it's your responsibility to deliver a message that contains information important to the reader. This section offers advice on delivering your message with impact.

11

Ask yourself the questions your reader will have: Who? What? When? Where? Why? How?

Newspaper reporters use the questioning technique to guide the reader through stories and provide the information the reader wants to know. Of course, not all the questions may apply to each message you write, so decide which ones add to your purpose of satisfying your reader's needs. (Before you know it, you'll be questioning everything from freedom to the law of gravity.)

Start by vertically listing Who? What? When? Where? Why? How? Ask yourself the questions the reader will have and answer them. For example, if you are calling a meeting, the reader will want to know the following:

Reader's Questions	Answers
Who will be there?	Bob, Grace, Samantha, and Joe.
What kind of meeting is it?	A conference call with the Chicago office.

When is the meeting?	March 3 at 11:00 a.m.
Where is the meeting?	Conference Room 2.
Why are we getting together?	To finalize details of the trade show.
How can I prepare?	Bring all our marketing materials.

Be sure to answer the questions specifically, not vaguely. For example, if you want the reader to send you something, do you want it sent by e-mail? Fax? Snail mail? Certified mail? Overnight? Return receipt?

> Using the questioning technique is critical when sending e-mails. Many people read messages on hand-held computers and have limited viewing space. Give them answers to their questions in one short paragraph. (If you're attaching a document, use this technique to summarize the attachment.)

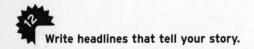

Write headlines that tell your story.

Newspapers and magazines use headlines to tell their stories and to direct the reader to what's important. Headlines can make or break a story. Here's a perfect example: Hal Prince, the noted Broadway producer, was interviewed on television. The commentator asked Mr. Prince how he knows when a show is a flop or a success. Mr. Prince answered something like this: "The morning after the show opens, I open the newspaper and read the headlines. The headlines make or break the show."

Headlines are powerful, and you can add that same power to all your writing. It's important to remember that people don't read; they scan. You can grab your reader's attention and deliver your key points quickly and effectively using headlines—just as editors do in a newspaper. In the following example, notice how the headlines tell the story.

Evacuation drills

Beginning next month, ABC Company will be conducting evacuation drills throughout the building.

Monday, June 9, at 10:00 a.m.

Next Monday you will hear a whooping alarm and the following announcement: "An evacuation drill will begin in the next few minutes. This is only a drill but it requires full participation. Employees will be asked to proceed to the nearest stairway, but not to leave the building."

Find emergency routes on bulletin boards

Emergency exit routes are posted on the bulletin boards throughout the building. When you hear the alarm, proceed to the nearest stairway exit and wait for the all-clear signal.

Here are some headlines you can use in your documents to call out what's important:

Action requested
Action required
Next step
Meeting information
    Date:
    Time:
    Place:
Deadline: [date]
Effective: [date]

Sequence the headlines strategically.

One of your challenges as a writer is to be mindful of where to put your key issue. The secret to writing effective documents and getting the results you want is to sequence your information for maximum impact. (You identified the reader's attitude in Tip 5.)

- For a *responsive or neutral reader,* put the key issue at the beginning of the document—perhaps it can serve as the subject line.

- For an *unresponsive reader,* cushion the key issue between buffers—a positive opening and friendly closing.

There are times you want to deliver a message to an unresponsive reader that packs a punch (for example, someone's account is long past due and you're threatening legal action). However, most times the message isn't that harsh.

When you must say no or disappoint the reader, you need special planning. Remember that your intention is to maintain goodwill. Here are some things to try:

- **Offer options.** A friend received a letter from a major university denying her daughter the financial aid she requested. The letter started, "I'm sorry to let you know that we can't. . ." When my friend called the university, she found out that there were other financial aid options to pursue.

  Instead of saying no, the letter might have said, "Although we can't grant you the financial aid you requested, we'd like to let you know of other funding options to pursue." That would have maintained goodwill.

- **Give an explanation.** Don't tell someone "It's company policy." Readers don't care about your policies. However, they do understand logical reasoning. Following is a letter I wrote for an insurance company explaining why the company couldn't pay for cosmetic surgery:

"Thank you for choosing <company> as your insurance provider. We know you have choices and are delighted you chose us. We'd love to say yes to everyone who wants an elective procedure. But if we did, we wouldn't have the funds to say yes to everyone who *needs* a procedure. We are confident that you'll understand. Please be assured that if you ever need a procedure, we'll be right there for you. Once again, thanks for choosing <company> as your provider."

- **Change the order.** Don't start with the bad news. Open with a buffer that's upbeat, and close on a friendly note. Put the bad news in the middle. You may even consider a neutral subject line, such as "Policy No. 6138."

- **Get creative.** It's not always appropriate to get creative, but here are two times creativity worked well:

My financial planner sent me a letter during a long economic downturn. It showed a line graph of how the stock market rebounded after the last two severe downturns. That was a very creative way to let clients know they shouldn't panic. Things typically get better.

I wrote an annual report for a company that had a bad year due to economic conditions. To counter the numbers, I generously peppered the report with testimonials from customers, many of which were very recognizable company names. The subtle message was that, despite bad numbers beyond our control, we're solid.

Don't get it right; get it written.

SHERYL LINDSELL-ROBERTS

You write and edit with different parts of your brain. If you try to do both at the same time, you may get a cranial traffic jam. Therefore, when you write the draft, try to express yourself without being critical of the results. Censor yourself later. Your task when writing the draft is to transfer your thoughts from your head to the computer (or paper).

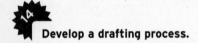

Develop a drafting process.

When you write a draft, don't wait for inspiration. Treat the draft as you would any on-the-job task. Just do it. Here are some suggestions to help you get started:

- **Create a comfortable environment.** If possible, create an environment that encourages concentration. If you try to write between phone calls and walk-in visitors, you'll be distracted. It takes time to reorganize your thoughts after each interruption.

- **Get all your stuff together.** Have all your supplies and source material handy. When you have to stop to look for things, it breaks your train of thought and you get derailed.

- **Set attainable goals.** Your goal can be to write for 15 to 30 minutes. It can be to expand one or two headlines. Write continually until your goal is met, no matter how good or bad your writing seems to be. The point is to keep writing.

- **Stay focused.** Once you create a comfortable environment, have your stuff ready, and set goals, you're ready to start drafting.

- **Start with the headline that's the easiest to fill in.** You may have heard the story of the aspiring novelist who kept rewriting the opening sentence. She never got beyond the first sentence because she didn't have structure. By planning and writing the headlines in advance, you have that much-needed structure.

Once the headlines are done, writing the draft is somewhat like filling in the blanks. Think of the headlines as bones that need meat. Start with the headline that's the easiest to develop. Then go to the second easiest. *Your reader will never know where you started.*

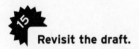

Revisit the draft.

After you finish writing the draft, get some distance. It's hard to be objective about your work when you're too close to it. Following are some tips for getting distance when you're pressed for time: Put your feet up and clear your mind, go for a short walk, get a cup of coffee, return telephone calls, pat yourself on the back. Even a 5- to 10-minute break will make a difference.

Now it's time to revisit your draft. You're not proofreading yet; you're just fine-tuning. Start with major changes, such as adding, deleting, or amending sections. Ask yourself these questions:

- **Are the headlines action-packed?** If not, pump them up for greater impact.

Action-packed:	Confirming Thursday's staff meeting
Actionless:	Meeting

Action-packed:	Rick Smith takes new position as of 12/5
Actionless:	Rick

- **Did I use paragraphs appropriately?** A *paragraph* is a group of sentences that develops a single idea in support of the headline.

Start each paragraph with a *topic sentence* that supplies the direction of the sentences to follow. *Limit paragraphs to eight lines of text*, and always leave a line space between each paragraph.

- **Did I explain the problem or situation clearly?** Your wording must be clear so the reader understands the significance of the problem, solution, or conclusion.

Clear:	Ted's supervisor couldn't make the meeting. The airport was closed because of the storm.
Unclear:	Ted's supervisor said he couldn't make the meeting because of the weather. (Who couldn't make the meeting, Ted or his supervisor? Why was the weather significant?)

- **Should I resequence?** After you write the draft, you may find it makes sense to resequence some of your headlines and paragraphs for greater impact. (Check out Tip 13 for more about sequencing.) Consider these questions:

  Do the headlines tell the story?
  Do they deliver my message strategically?
  Did I deliver good or neutral news first?
  Did I cushion bad news?

- **Does the reader need background information?** Most backgrounds are dull, and people don't read them. Include only the information the reader needs to know—not information she is already familiar with. (Check out Tip 2 for more about what the reader *needs to know*.)

- **Did I provide closure?** Check out Tip 6 to determine the action item. Do you want the reader to call you, attend a meeting, send something, write a report, do nothing?

*Gutenberg made everybody a reader. Xerox made
everybody a publisher.*

MARSHALL McLUHAN
Canadian educator and author

Visuals are attention-getters that communicate information at a glance.
They provide a subtle, unconscious signal. For example, think of the way
numbers visually impact documents. Should you write "half ton," "½
ton," "0.50 ton," or "1,000 pounds"? It all depends on the emphasis. When
you want to play down the weight, "1,000 pounds" is a better choice than
"half ton."

When a message has visual impact, it attracts attention, invites read-
ership, and establishes your credibility even before you state your case.
Here's what visual impact will do for your documents:

- **Spark immediate interest.** Visuals unlock doors of meaning.
  Because of their size, shape, color, and arrangement, good visuals
  are dramatic and maintain interest.

- **Organize information.** A good visual design breaks the message
  into manageable, bite-sized chunks, making it easy for the reader
  to find the key pieces of information. It helps the reader concen-
  trate on one idea at a time.

- **Emphasize what's important.** If you create a hierarchy of information, your reader can separate major points from supporting
  ones. In today's harried world where people are pulling their hair
  out because of tight schedules, your reader will appreciate your
  logical sequencing of ideas.

- **Increase understanding by simplifying concepts.** Where a verbal
  description states ideas, a visual shows ideas. Visuals are especially
  helpful in explaining a technical process to a nontechnical reader.

- **Condense a lot of information into a relatively small space.** You can condense large amounts of statistical or financial data—over many weeks, months, and even years—into one compact visual.

16

Allow ample white space.

White space refers to all areas on the page where there is neither type nor graphics. White space is a key ingredient in visual design for paper and electronic documents. People take it for granted that white space is something a document should have, but they don't always know why. White space makes the document inviting and approachable by providing contrast and a resting place for the reader's eyes. Here are some tips for using white space effectively:

- Maintain 1- to 1½-inch top, bottom, and side margins to create a visual frame around printed text and graphics. Leave the default margins for electronic copy.

- Keep equal distance from left to right and from top to bottom in letters.

- Limit paragraphs to eight lines of text. Not sentences, lines.

- Leave a line space between each paragraph to help the reader see each paragraph as a separate unit.

- Leave a line space between each item in a bulleted or numbered list when each item contains three lines or more. Also, leave a line space above and below the list.

Questions about font size and style typically come up at my workshops. Times Roman 12, or a comparable serif font, works well for paper documents. That's why word processing programs typically default to Times 12. It's fine to use Times 11 if you're pressed for space, but anything smaller may be difficult to read. Ariel 10, or a comparable sans serif font, works well for electronic documents. That's why e-mail programs typically default to Ariel 10.

17 Use headlines, subheads, and sidelines.

Each headline and subhead serves as a guidepost, enabling the reader to get the gist of a message by skimming the text. Here are some ways to present headlines and subheads:

- ALL CAPS
- Different Font
- First Letter Caps
- **ALL CAPS BOLD**
- SMALL CAPS
- First Letter Caps Underscored

Sidelines—captions running down the left column—offer an alternative to headlines and subheads. You often see sidelines in resumes, user manuals, data sheets, agendas, fliers, or any document where the reader needs to scan the left column to find the key information at a glance. The following *Before* and *After* examples show how you can use sidelines to help the reader find information quickly.

Before: With bullets, critical information gets lost.

> - The agency developed services and products for the 401(k) offering at the Dime Savings Bank. The work involved marketing strategy and naming architecture.
>
> - The agency provided direct marketing and advertising programs to Condor Bank, enabling the bank to reach customers and businesses outside of its home base.

After: With sidelines, critical information stands out.

Dime Savings Bank	The agency developed services and products for the 401(k) offering at the Dime Savings Bank. The work involved marketing strategy and naming architecture.
Condor Bank	The agency provided direct marketing and advertising programs to Condor Bank, enabling the bank to reach customers and businesses outside of its home base.

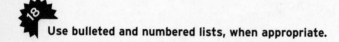

18

Use bulleted and numbered lists, when appropriate.

Lists help the reader focus on important information by breaking out key items from the stream of the sentence. Lists draw the reader's attention to critical points. Be sure you don't weaken your impact by making an entire page one long laundry list of bulleted or numbered items. If you do, nothing stands out. As a rule of thumb, if you have more than six key items, break them into sections:

Countries Visited	*Countries Visited*
Italy	Europe
Spain	*Italy*
Japan	*Spain*
France	*France*
Germany	*Germany*
China	Asia
Korea	*Japan*
	China
	Korea

There's a difference between a bulleted list and a numbered list. Use a bulleted list when rank or sequence aren't important. To level the playing field and de-emphasize priority, consider presenting a bulleted list in alphabetical order.

Bulleted list indicates everything is of equal importance.

Please send us a list of the following:

- Cost
- Tooling
- Weight saved

If sequence is important, use numbers. In the following example, you are letting the reader know that cost is the most important item on the list.

Numbered list indicates order of importance.

Please send us a list of the following:

1. Cost
2. Tooling
3. Weight saved

 You also use a numbered list to show a sequence of events or steps in a process.

19 Use charts, tables, and graphs, when appropriate.

Charts and tables are a great way to make your point effectively, and there are more opportunities than you may think to use them.

In the following charts, the writer tries to show the differences between three processes. As you can see, in the *Before* example she uses bullets excessively and the differences between the processes do not stand out. In the *After* example, she takes the same information and turns it into a readable chart that highlights the differences very clearly.

Before: Differences are hidden.

Injection Molding	Blow Molding	Extrusion
• Increases MFI/reduces resin viscosity	• Increases MFI/reduces resin viscosity	• Increases MFI/reduces resin viscosity
• Provides for quicker cycles	• Provides for quicker cycles	• Allows easy mold/die release
• Allows easy mold/die release	• Allows easy mold/die release	• Improves dispersion of color and filler
• Allows for easy cavity fill	• Improves dispersion of color and filler	• Eliminates stress and flow marks

After: Differences are obvious.

Benefit	Injection Molding	Blow Molding	Extrusion
Increases MFI/reduces resin viscosity	✔	✔	✔
Provides for quicker cycles	✔	✔	
Allows easy mold/die release	✔	✔	✔
Improves dispersion of color and filler		✔	✔
Allows for easy cavity fill	✔	✔	
Eliminates stress and flow marks	✔	✔	✔
Improves cosmetic surfaces	✔	✔	✔
Reduces sink marks	✔	✔	✔
Reduces coefficient of friction	✔	✔	✔
Provides clean parts, ready for finishing	✔	✔	✔
Cleans continuous extrusion		✔	✔
Eliminates residue from barrel and screw	✔	✔	✔
Uses less energy	✔	✔	✔

When you have a long table, consider alternately shading rows.

You can gather data and prepare a chart to display findings, identify opportunities, update data, show progress, or more. Many software programs can help you prepare charts, tables, and graphics in a jiffy. Keep these tips in mind when you prepare charts and graphs:

- **Write a descriptive title.** Place the title above the chart or graph.

- **Use an appropriate scale.** For example, if the financial range in question is from $100,000 to $200,000, don't show a scale from $100,000 to $500,000.

- **Create a legend.** If the chart isn't self-explanatory, the legend will explain the symbols that appear in the chart.

- **Keep the design simple.** Eliminate any information your readers don't need to know.

- **Prepare a separate graph or chart for each point.** If you try to squeeze too much information on one chart or graph, you defeat your purpose of making it simple to read.

- **Choose the best type of chart for your purpose.** Here are some commonly used charts and graphs and their functions:

Type of Chart	What It Shows
Pie	Percentages that total 100
Line	Trends, changes of one or more variables over time, or relationships between sets of numbers
Bar	Comparisons between categories or among quantities
Histogram	Relative frequency of occurrences, central tendencies, or variability among data sets
Pareto	Vital information as distinguished from trivial information
Gantt	Coordinate resources and activities

When preparing graphics for an international audience, be mindful of how the graphics may translate. Ask someone from your reader's country to take a look at them. Following are some things to consider:

- **Be sure your graphics don't have any religious significance.** For example, in the US a red cross symbolizes first aid. In Muslim countries a cross may suggest Christianity.

- **Understand how your reader will interpret the graphics.** For example, the languages of North America and Europe are read from left to right. Arabic and Hebrew, however, are read from right to left.

- **Use neutral colors.** For example, red is associated with happiness in China, but red graphics might suggest danger in the US.

Although charts, tables, and graphs are appropriate for many situations, consider using numbers told in story form to underscore a specific point. What can be more specific than "225 out of 250 people chose . . ." or ". . . is 78 percent more effective"? Studies show that when presented with stories as opposed to a display of numerical data, twice as many readers remember the point afterwards.

20 Use color judiciously.

We use color to interpret the meaning of what we see. Color adds visual impact so we can separate the ripe from the unripe, match our clothes, enjoy flowers, and so on. You can use color to create a mood and give a real-world look to the written word. Use color for headlines or anything you want to stand out. The following chart can help you use color to create the impact you want.

Color	Associations Evoked
White	Sanitary, pure, clean, honest
Black	Serious, heavy, death, elegant
Red	Stop, danger, excitement, heat
Dark Blue	Calming, stable, trustworthy, mature
Light Blue	Masculine, youthful, cool
Green	Growth, organic, go, positive
Gray	Neutral, cool, mature, integrity
Brown	Organic, wholesome, unpretentious
Yellow	Positive, cautious, emotional
Gold	Elegant, stable, rich, conservative
Orange	Emotional, organic, positive
Purple	Contemporary, youthful
Pink	Feminine, warm, youthful, calming
Pastels	Sensitive, feminine, soft
Metallics	Wealthy, elegant, lasting

TONE

There is no quicker way for two executives to get out of touch with each other than to retire to the seclusion of their offices and write each other notes.

R. ALEC MACKENZIE
American management consultant

Tone is the sound you make on paper. When you speak to someone in person, much of what you say is interpreted through nonverbal cues such as facial expressions, gestures, tone of voice, inflections, eye contact, movements, and so on. Body language isn't possible with the written word, so it's critical to choose your words carefully.

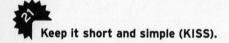

Keep it short and simple (KISS).

Keeping it short and simple is the quintessence of great writing. (KISS is an acronym that's been used to mean "Keep it simple, stupid." I prefer to think it stands for "Keep it short and simple.") In either event, the operative word is *simple*.

Time and *Newsweek* are written at high-school reading level. *The Wall Street Journal* and *The New York Times* are written at 10th-grade level. *USA Today* writes for 7th-grade level, and *People* magazine for 6th-grade level. Classic novels such as *The Catcher in the Rye* and *Moby-Dick* are at 8th-grade level. And Hemingway rarely used words that had more than two syllables.

Keep it short and simple by limiting your sentences to no more than 25 words. Columnist Ann Landers, World War II correspondent Ernie Pyle, and Sir Winston Churchill all shared a typical sentence length of 15 words. Even the sentences in Churchill's blood-sweat-and-tears radio speeches and his journalism from the Boer War averaged 15 words.

Keep it short

The shortest letter on record may have been received by Victor Hugo in 1862. Hugo had sent his publisher a letter asking what they thought of his manuscript *Les Miserables*. The publisher's response said it all:

Keep it simple

Here's a letter by Cornelius Vanderbilt, a very wealthy and ruthless industrialist. It's short and simple with not one wasted word:

> You have undertaken to cheat me. I won't sue you for the law is too slow. I'll ruin you.

Whether a sentence is long or short, it should be concise. *Concise* isn't the opposite of *long*; it's the opposite of *wordy*. Even a 10-word sentence may be verbose. Eliminate every word that doesn't add value. Consider these examples:

Concise: Please confirm delivery of the HCE exchangers (5%/9%RD) needed by July 1, 20—. (13 words)

Wordy: We wish to request that you notify us if the HCE exchangers (5%/9%RD) will be ready to be shipped on or before July 1, 20—. (25 words)

Concise:	Please let us know by April 15 if you plan to attend the May 2 workshop. Enrollment is light. (19 words)
Wordy:	Due to the lack of enrollment and interest, we might find it necessary to cancel the workshop scheduled for May 2 at 2:30. We'll regret having to do this, so please be certain that you let us know by April 15 if you're desirous of attending. (46 words)

Avoid expressions on steroids

Never pad your sentences with words that don't add value. Here are just a few phrases to use and avoid:

Instead of ...	*Use ...*
came to an agreement	agreed
conducted experiments	experimented
give an indication	show
completely opposite	opposite
new breakthrough	breakthrough
honest truth	truth

Write in plain language

In 1998, President Clinton issued an executive memo requiring agencies to write in plain language. Although there's no single definition of plain language (also called plain English), it refers to writing that's easy to read, easy to understand, and easy to use. Notice the difference in the following documents, taken from www.plainlanguage.gov.

207.1 Introduction

For JSC emergencies, call x33333. For Ellington Field emergencies, call x47231. For White Sands Test Facility emergencies, call x5911. Off site, call 911. The first priority of a person on site who observes an outbreak of fire or other situation that constitutes an emergency is to immediately contact the emergency phone numbers for assistance. In many cases, immediate evacuation of a facility or area may be necessary. Notification and evacuation are to have priority over attempts by untrained personnel to combat the emergency. It is JSC policy that employees not "fight" fires that cannot be safely extinguished with a hand held fire extinguisher unless such employees are certified members of a fire brigade or any formally organized fire department. Employees should not try to fight a fire unless they first notify the fire department, are trained in fire extinguisher use, and can safely extinguish the fire.

207.2 Purpose

The purpose of this chapter is to provide guidelines for reporting an emergency and details what shall be contained in emergency action plans that give information and guidance to building personnel after an incident has been discovered.

207.3 Scope

This chapter applies to the reporting of medical and fire emergencies and emergencies involving a hazardous substance anywhere on JSC property, including Ellington Field and the Sonny Carter Training Facility. Also included are guidelines for general emergency action plans in each of the JSC and Ellington Field buildings.

This could be you . . .

Several people could have been exposed to a toxic gas because they left their buildings after the gas release. They didn't know what to do.

A fire in an area with hazardous materials burned longer than it should have while firefighters tried to find out if they could use water on the fire. Little planning had been done for this emergency. A computer area was flooded when a water line broke. The emergency plan didn't cover water leaks.

1. Who must follow this chapter?

You must follow this chapter if you work at JSC or a JSC field site. If you are a supervisor, facility manager, or director, Paragraph 16 of this chapter lists your responsibilities.

2. What does this chapter cover?

This chapter tells you what to do in an emergency of any kind and what emergency planning JSC must do.

Emergency Action

3. What emergencies must I report?

You must report any emergency that you see. This includes any fire, no matter how small. Report fires that have been extinguished. They may still be smoldering and could reignite.

Remember, your emergency numbers are: x33333 at JSC, x44444 at Ellington Field, 911 at any off-site location, and x5911 at White Sands Test Facility.

You must call your emergency number if you see an emergency.

You must keep the emergency scene as undisturbed as possible. If you don't, valuable evidence for the investigators could be destroyed.

Use positive words, rather than negative words.

Presenting yourself as an optimist is a winning strategy. Let the reader know what you can and will do, not what you can't and won't do. Using positive words engages the reader's goodwill and makes your tone more inviting.

Positive: We can charge orders of $25 or more.
Negative: We can't charge orders of less than $25.

Positive: Participation for January remained at 45 percent.
Negative: Participation for the month of January did not increase. It remained at 45 percent.

 I recently wrote a user manual for a client who invented an electrical appliance. He was adamant about putting on the cover, "This is no more dangerous than a hair dryer." I convinced him that we shouldn't use the word *dangerous* because it would glare at readers like a neon sign. Instead I wrote, "This is as safe as a hair dryer."

When you do write something negative, do it strategically. For example, the following marketing message pinpoints the pain of the prospective customer:

- Is your bottom line impacted because you can't measure the effectiveness of plans and employees across your enterprise?

- Are you troubled because you don't know if you're paying too much or too little in commissions?

- Are you fighting constant fires trying to manage your commission spreadsheet farm?

If you answer yes to even one of these questions, you need to put the right tools in the hands of the right people at the right time.

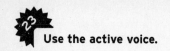

Use the active voice.

Voice is the grammatical term that refers to whether the subject of the sentence performs or receives the action of the verb. You can make your writing more alive and interesting by using the active voice whenever possible. When you write a sentence in the active voice, you make the subject the "doer." (In a sentence that is a command, you can infer the subject or doer from the context—you won't see the subject, but it's there. The subject is the person to whom you are speaking.)

Active:	Jim and Sally share the printer.
Passive:	The printer is shared by Jim and Sally.

Active:	Please turn off the lights before you leave the building in the evening. (Doer is inferred.)
Passive:	The lights should be turned off before the building is closed for the night.

The doer doesn't need to be a person. It can be a place or thing.

Active:	Minnesota experienced a warm winter this year.
Passive:	A warm winter was experienced by Minnesota this year.

Active:	The new software requires an extra step in the workflow.
Passive:	An extra step in the workflow is required by the new software.

When you write a sentence in the passive voice, you make the subject the receiver of the action. Passive sentences are often dull and weak, but at times they can be used strategically. In the following examples, the passive voice is effective:

- The law firm was established in the early 1900s. (You want to focus on the action, not the actor.)

■ Mistakes were made. (You are protecting the people who made the mistakes.)

> Researchers often use the passive voice when reporting scientific research because they want to focus on the research results rather than on the person who performed the tests. However, you can use the active voice by writing "Test results show . . ."

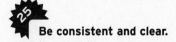

Use *you* and *your* more than *I, me, we,* and *us.*

Have you ever gone to a party and been cornered by a bore who talked incessantly about himself? It's pretty annoying. The next time you see that bore, would you be anxious to spend more time with him? No, you'd probably find a tall plant to hide behind. When appropriate, use terms that represent your reader, rather than yourself.

Reader focus:	Your department will be getting a new accountant.
Writer focus:	I'll be hiring a new accountant for your department.

Reader focus:	As one of Mason & Green's catalog customers, you can now use your credit card to place your order by phone.
Writer focus:	We want you to know that we appreciate having you as one of Mason & Green's catalog customers. We have decided that we can make catalog shopping a lot easier by issuing you one of our credit cards. With this card, we can take your orders by phone.

Be consistent and clear.

Following are guidelines for maintaining consistency and clarity:

■ **Use consistent wording.** For example, if you make reference to a "user manual," don't later call it a "reference manual" or "user guide." Your reader may think you are referring to separate documents.

As with every rule or guideline, there are exceptions. I found an exception when I wrote an online press release for my e-mail Webinar. Needing to anticipate key search words for a large audience, I used *email* and *e-mail*, *online* and *on-line*, and *training* and *workshop*. These inconsistencies gave me the best chance of attracting the widest audience.

- **Use repetition strategically.** Many people go out of their way to avoid repeating words; however, repetition is appropriate in some instances.

  Repetition can make a sentence read cohesively. During Franklin Roosevelt's inaugural address he said, "We have nothing to fear but fear itself." That statement would have been much less powerful and much less memorable if he had said, "We have nothing to fear but alarm itself."

  Repeat key words when you want to drive a point home: "See the whites get whiter. See the reds get redder. See the blues get bluer."

- **Avoid ambiguity.** Don't use *should* or *may* when there are no options. "Don't smoke when operating this equipment" is definite. "You shouldn't smoke when operating this equipment" expresses a hint of uncertainty.

- **The words *and* and *but* are not interchangeable.** *But* communicates a negative message, an obstacle, a hitch, or something problematic you didn't expect. *And* communicates a positive message, something good that you expected.

Positive:	Tom was new to consulting and outperformed expectations. (His good performance was expected.)
Negative:	Tom was new to consulting but outperformed expectations. (His good performance was a surprise.)

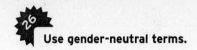

Use gender-neutral terms.

Gender neutrality is often a matter of rewording the sentence. The examples that follow show a number of ways to say the same thing.

Wordy:	Each person did his/her work quietly.
Awkward:	Each person did their work quietly.
Acceptable:	Each person did the work quietly.
Acceptable:	Each person worked quietly.
Acceptable:	Everyone worked quietly.

Or, consider turning a singular sentence into a plural sentence.

Singular:	Each student must file his/her application by June 5. He/she should state . . .
Plural:	All students should file their applications by June 5. They should state . . .

When you refer to people by job descriptions, be aware of gender-neutral terms. Following are some to consider:

Rather than saying . . .	*Try . . .*
cameraman	cinematographer
chairman, chairwoman	chairperson, chair, moderator
clergyman	member of the clergy
delivery boy	delivery person, messenger
fireman	firefighter
forefather	ancestor
insurance man	insurance agent
layman	nonprofessional
man-made	synthetic
mankind	humanity, human race
newsman	reporter, journalist
policeman, policewoman	police officer

Rather than saying …	*Try …*
postman	mail carrier, letter carrier
repairman, repairwoman	service technician
salesman, saleswoman	salesperson, sales representative
spokesman	spokesperson
steward, stewardess	flight attendant
weatherman	meteorologist
workman	worker

27 Use industry-related jargon appropriately.

Industry-related jargon is specialized "shop talk" unique to people in an industry. When writing to people in your industry who understand these terms, it makes no sense to water down the language. Doing so may damage the integrity of the document and insult the reader. When you write to people outside the industry, however, avoid jargon. The tone may become tangled in abstract words that the reader may view as exclusionary. When you include industry-related jargon, consider your reader.

- Explain the term at first mention. For example, "Bob is the subject matter expert (SME)." Thereafter, SME may stand alone because you already explained it.

- If you have many industry-related terms, include a glossary at the end of the document for easy reference. Also consider a glossary for a website that may have lots of industry-related terms.

28 Think seriously about being funny.

Will Rogers once said, "Everything is funny as long as it is happening to somebody else." What's funny to one reader may be insulting to another. Even among friends, humor can be cutting. George Bernard Shaw once sent tickets to his latest play to his good friend Winston Churchill. Mr. Shaw included this note: "Here are two tickets to my new play. Bring a friend—if you have one." Mr. Churchill returned the tickets with this note: "Sorry, I'm unable to attend opening night. Please send me tickets for the second performance—if there is one."

When used properly, however, humor can make a technical subject more enjoyable and easier to understand. Here's how Lewis Thomas handled humor in *The Lives of a Cell*:

> Ants are so much like human beings as to be an embarrassment. They farm fungi, raise aphids as livestock, launch armies into wars, use chemical sprays to alarm and confuse enemies, capture slaves. The families of weaver ants engage in child labor, holding their larvae like shuttles to spin out the thread that sews the leaves together for their fungus gardens. They exchange information ceaselessly. They do everything but watch television.

When you speak, you constantly punctuate with your voice and your body language. When you write, you also make a sound in the reader's head. It can be a dull mumble, a joyful sound, a shy whisper, a throb of passion. Punctuation is one of the most significant tools for giving your document feeling. Following are some ways to create your voice:

- **Question marks** automatically signal interactivity because they get the reader involved. When the question is thought provoking, it makes a good opener that compels the reader to think a certain way.

- **Exclamation points** create excitement. (Two exclamation points, however, are weak, because they betray the sense of excitement.)

- **Colons** push the reader into what follows. They propel the concept of the incompleteness of what's been said before.

- **Dashes** used around parenthetical text—instead of commas—accentuate what's enclosed in the dashes. "Instead of commas" yells.

- **Parentheses** used around parenthetical text (instead of commas) downplay what's enclosed in the parentheses. "Instead of commas" whispers.

When you write to people you know or on behalf of people you know (supervisors or managers, for example), look at what they write to understand how they communicate. Mimic their personality style. Following is a chart that offers suggestions for writing to people who are dominant, influential, steady, and compliant:

Style	Traits	Best Methods of Presentation
Dominant	• Need to direct • Results oriented • Motivated by challenge and power	• Be direct and to the point; stick to business • Provide win-win situations • Focus on bottom line; offer results without overusing data
Influential	• Need to interact • People oriented • Motivated by recognition and involvement	• Use a positive introduction to break the ice • Highlight benefits and generate excitement • Show samples, if appropriate
Steady	• Need to serve • Cooperation oriented • Motivated by stability and appreciation	• Use a step-by-step process • Leave time for recapping and review • Attach supporting materials
Compliant	• Need to comply to high standards • Quality oriented • Motivated by standards and desired expectations	• Avoid new ideas; stick to proven facts • Be detailed, and provide statistics • Use lots of graphs and charts • Examine arguments from all sides

*How would you like a job where, if you made a mistake, a
big red light goes on and 18,000 people boo?*

JACQUES PLANTE
former National Hockey League goalie

Proofreading and editing are akin to quality control. In manufacturing,
quality control is making sure merchandise is free from defects. In writing, it means making sure your document is free from errors.
Proofreading refers to locating errors. *Editing* refers to amending text,
from changing content to modifying paragraphs, sentences, and words.

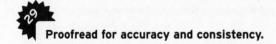

Proofread for accuracy and consistency.

What would you do if you went to a restaurant and the menu included
"white whine," "soap of the day," "baked zits," and "turkey coffee"? You'd
probably run. You don't want your readers to run visually. Proofread
until your eyeballs hurt. Here are a few simple guidelines:

- **Check the accuracy of all names, including middle initials and
  titles.** Do you spell the recipient's name *Carol* or *Carole*? And
  don't assume you know the sex of a person by the name. Carroll
  O'Connor is a man and Stevie Nicks is a woman.

- **Confirm company designations.** Does the company use "Co.,"
  "Company," "Inc.," "Incorporated"?

- **Double-check all numbers.** It's easy to transpose them.

- **Keep an eye out for misused or misspelled homophones (words
  that sound the same but are spelled differently).** Know the difference between *principal* and *principle*, *capital* and *capitol*, *station-
  ary* and *stationery*, and other homophones.

- **Be on the alert for small words that you repeat or misspell.** It's easy to write *it* instead of *is* and not realize it.

- **Check dates against the calendar to make sure the day and date coincide.** If you write Monday, May 3, be sure May 3 is a Monday.

Check, double-check, and triple-check spelling, grammar, and punctuation. *Don't turn on your computer and turn off your brain.* Notice the difference in the following when you change the punctuation:

Execution: impossible to be pardoned.
Execution impossible: to be pardoned.

After I dressed and ate, my parents . . .
After I dressed and ate my parents, . . .

 My client, the public relations director of a large, multinational corporation, tells this story: She sent out a very critical e-mail message to members of her firm in North America, Europe, and Asia. At the end of the message she signed her name and her title, Pubic Relations Director. (She left the *l* out of *public*.) Be sure to proofread everything, not just the obvious.

30 Edit for content.

Here are some suggestions to keep in mind when editing:

- **Be sure your sentences and paragraphs flow smoothly.**

- **Sequence your document so it tells the story.** Check out Tip 13 for how to sequence information.

- **Look for omissions.** For example, did you remember to attach the document you mentioned in your e-mail message?

- **Reword any sentences you have to read more than once.** If you have trouble understanding them, the reader will also.

- **Print out the message and read the hard copy.** Despite the hours we spend on our computers, we're still more used to the printed word. We tend to see errors on paper we missed on the screen.

- **Read the document aloud.** Reading aloud, even in a mumble, will slow you down so you see what's actually there.

- **Have someone else read it.** When a document is important, have someone else read it.

Before you send out any document, use the following checklist:

BUSINESS/TECHNICAL WRITING CHECKLIST

☐ My subject line and headlines are informative, to spark my reader's interest.

☐ My message is sequenced for the needs of my reader.

☐ My document has strong visual impact:

    ☐ Ample white space throughout

    ☐ 1- to $1\frac{1}{2}$-inch margins on the top, bottom, and sides

    ☐ Sentences limited to 20–25 words

    ☐ Paragraphs limited to 8 lines

    ☐ Bulleted and numbered lists, when appropriate

    ☐ Tables and charts, when appropriate.

☐ The tone is appropriate:

    ☐ Reader-focused

    ☐ Short and to the point (KISS)

    ☐ Positive words

    ☐ Active voice

    ☐ "You" approach.

☐ Spelling, grammar, and punctuation are correct.

☐ I didn't lay my cup down and leave coffee stains on the paper.

PART TWO

Moving Forward

**A WIDE
ARRAY OF
BUSINESS
DOCUMENTS**

Several years ago I received a phone call from the editor of a leading business publication. He asked me if I knew the dollar amount that businesses are losing each year because of poor business writing. I thought for a while. I had never come across such a figure. *Businesses are losing billions of dollars a year because of poor business writing and they don't even realize it.*

- When you submit a *proposal* and don't get the contract, do you immediately think that the contract went to a lower bidder or to someone who knew someone on the inside? If so, take a look at the quality of your writing. Perhaps the proposal was disorganized, poorly written, or incomplete.

- When you prepare a *sales or marketing brochure* and it doesn't generate revenue, do you blame it on an inept sales force or on a slumping economy? If so, take a look at the quality of your writing. Perhaps your marketing message didn't differentiate you from your competitors.

- When you prepare an *instruction manual* and your help line rings off the wall, do you think your customers are too lazy to read? That may be the case. But, take a look at the quality of your writing. Perhaps the instructions were unclear or poorly organized.

I could go on and on about businesses losing money because of poor business writing; I hear it from my clients regularly. After that phone call from the editor, I came up with the tag line for my business: *You make more dollars when you make more sense.*™

After you go through Part One—and it's essential that you do before you dive into Part Two—you're ready to tackle any writing project. Part Two addresses a wide variety of business documents commonly used by working professionals.

ABSTRACTS

*The factory of the future will have only two
employees, a man and a dog. The man will be there
to feed the dog. The dog will be there to keep the man
from touching the equipment.*

WARREN BENNIS
American educator and business writer

Abstracts are typically 150 to 250 words long. They cover the main points of a longer document using the same level of technical language. They are unlike executive summaries, which cover the information in greater detail, and are often written in nontechnical language. (See Executive Summaries, beginning on page 83.)

An abstract is somewhat like a preview intended to whet your readers' appetites, similar to a movie trailer that helps viewers determine if they want to see the full feature. People often read abstracts to determine whether the longer report is of interest. Here are some ways in which abstracts may be used:

- For distribution at trade shows, conferences, or seminars to generate interest in a product, service, or presentation.

- To provide managers (inside or outside the company) with a thumbnail version of a topic.

- In journals with information on how to find the longer document.

 Before you start writing your abstract, be certain you've gone through the process in Part One.

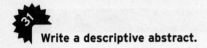

Write a descriptive abstract.

Descriptive abstracts are generally a few sentences. They're informal and may merely be a table of contents in sentence format. They don't have a headline that says "Abstract." For example, the following descriptive abstract from a user manual explains in just two sentences what the manual is about.

> This user manual describes the commands, statements, functions, and uses of Wonderblast software. This software runs on any PC or Mac.

Write an informative abstract.

Informative abstracts summarize the key elements of a document. Sometimes readers will rely on the abstract alone as their primary source of information. Informative abstracts should include the following:

- Subject, scope, and purpose of the study
- A brief discussion of the methodology
- Results of the study
- Conclusions or recommendations, if any.

They should *not* include

- A detailed discussion of the methods used
- Illustrations, charts, tables, or bibliographical references
- Any information that does not also appear in the full text.

Abstracts can stand alone or be part of the longer text. When they stand alone, always let readers know where they can find the full document—in print and/or electronic form.

> *The best way to become acquainted with a subject*
> *is to write a book [or article] about it.*

BENJAMIN DISRAELI
British novelist and former prime minister of England

Writing an article under your byline is one of the most effective ways to promote yourself or your business. Don't be intimidated by the prospect of approaching a publisher. Editors are always on the lookout for good material and competent writers. Not all publications pay for articles or offer honorariums. The payoff is gaining new customers/clients or driving traffic to your website. Here's how to get mileage from your article:

- Create a link to the article on your website.
- Send copies to colleagues and clients.
- Send an e-mail blast to colleagues and clients.
- Attach a copy of the article to your resume.

If your topic is revolutionary or very controversial, you may face some obstacles in getting your article published. Editors aren't necessarily crusaders. Crusaders in the publishing world either receive journalism awards or find their golden futures behind them.

 Before you start writing your article, be certain you've gone through the process in Part One.

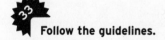
Follow the guidelines.

Publishers are bombarded with article submissions and only select a few. You know what publications people in your profession read. Contact these publications and ask for guidelines. Here's how to help tip the scales in your favor:

- Read several issues of your target publications to become familiar with the style and types of articles they publish.
- Write a descriptive title to intrigue your readers. (Lists are always popular, such as "10 Ways to . . ." or "12 Hot Tips for . . .")
- Include powerful headlines throughout the article.
- Use callout boxes to call attention to critical pieces of information.
- Use correct grammar, punctuation, and spelling.
- Limit your biographical information to six lines or less.

Unless you get paid a substantial fee, retain the rights to your article. If you submit the same article to several journals, consider making some changes. Modify the title and 25 percent of the text.

Write a meaningful and compelling title. There's no "right" title length, but you do want to lure the reader into reading your article.

- Ask yourself what title would catch your attention.
- Make a list of every word that applies to your topic.
- Understand the keyword(s) that a library or the Internet would use to find you.
- Try out different titles and run them by people whose opinions you trust.

34 Write a dynamite summary.

Some readers read only summaries, so use the summary to capture attention. Here are some tips:

- Include the *who*, *what*, *when*, *where*, *why*, and *how* just as journalists do.
- Write the summary as your first paragraph to get to the point quickly.

- Lure readers with the benefits of reading the entire article. Avoid wasted words such as "This article contains . . ." Focus on the *why*, not the *how*.

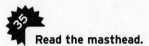

Read the masthead.

You find the masthead in the front part of the publication. It lists the publishers, editors, phone numbers or e-mail addresses, branch offices, board of reviewing editors, member societies, and other good stuff. At first glance you may notice that nearly everyone listed is an editor of some sort. If you can't determine the proper contact, call the publication and ask.

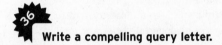

Write a compelling query letter.

A query letter (or cover letter) is the first thing an editor reads. The letter offers a clear indication of your writing style and thought process. Limit the letter to one page and suggest your title as a "working title." You don't need to send the article; you need to entice the editor to ask for it. Following are some tips for writing a query letter:

- Start with a hook—an attention grabber.
- Stress how you intend to approach the topic and develop it.
- Mention what photographs or other graphics (if any) you intend to send that will support your topic.
- Indicate why you're qualified to write the article. Attach a resume if you think it will strengthen your chances.

 Here's a cover letter I used to get an article published in a boating magazine:

Dear <editor>:

A favorite conversation among boaters is always boat names. Each boat owner likes to share how or why he named his boat. I thought <publication> would be an ideal place for boat owners to do just that.

Working Title: "What's in a Name: It's Absolute Lunar Sea"

I sent out questionnaires to boat owners and have accumulated dozens of funny and heartwarming stories. In addition, many boat owners sent high-quality photographs of their boats, showing the names. This article would make wonderful reading for the boaters in your audience.

Next step

Please let me know if you're interested in reading my 1500-word manuscript with a view toward publishing it. I look forward to hearing from you and sharing these wonderful stories with your readers.

Sincerely,

If your query letter doesn't get a response within a month, give the editor a call or drop him an e-mail. He's probably swamped with submissions and may not have read yours. By calling, you may help your query rise to the top.

If one publisher rejects you, keep sending your submission to others. A rejection isn't necessarily a rejection of your topic or your writing. It may merely mean that the topic isn't appropriate for that particular publication or the publication doesn't have that topic scheduled on its calendar.

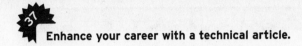

37

Enhance your career with a technical article.

There are several thousand technical, business, academic, scientific, and trade publications that engineers, scientists, and other specialized professionals use to tell peers and institutions about their work. Following are several benefits of getting a technical article published:

- Personal satisfaction
- Professional prestige
- An increase in your status as a technical expert
- Good publicity for you and your organization
- Helping others by contributing to a pool of technical knowledge.

As a technical expert, you don't need to write like Shakespeare. Publications have editors who polish manuscripts to make them more readable and more interesting. However, your article should be well-organized and neatly presented.

 For additional article-writing opportunities, consider the following:

- **E-zines (magazines published online).** E-zine publishers often include articles written by a guest author. At the end of the article you may be able to include your contact information. You probably won't get paid for an e-zine article, but your writing will gain exposure.

- **Company newsletters.** If your company publishes a newsletter, contribute an article. This is a great way to promote yourself and your department. Gather recent issues of the newsletter to become familiar with its style, tone, and subject matter.

*Doing business without advertising is like
winking at a girl in the dark. You know what
you are doing, but nobody else does.*

STEUART HENDERSON BRITT
American educator

Brochures let people know you are out there. They are something tangible you leave behind after a sales call, mail to a potential customer or client, or distribute at a trade show. Even though most businesses have websites, the printed piece is still king.

 Before you start writing your brochure, be certain you've gone through the process in Part One.

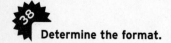

Determine the format.

This section concentrates on the bi-fold, tri-panel brochure. It's the most commonly used—an 8½-by-11 sheet folded twice to create three panels on each side, as shown on page 57. An advantage to this brochure is that it can be mailed in a standard #10 envelope. Here's how to use the panels wisely:

Front cover. Make the front cover visually appealing with just enough content to invite the reader to open the brochure and read more. The front cover should include (at the very least) your company name and logo. You may also include an applicable quote or tag line, as in the examples that follow.

Bi-fold, tri-panel brochure

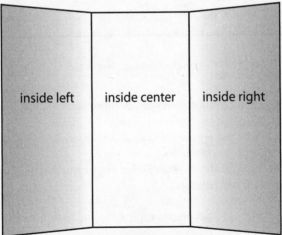

| inside flap | back cover | front cover |

Side 1

| inside left | inside center | inside right |

Side 2

For an architecture firm:

> That which we elect to surround ourselves with becomes the museum of our souls and the archives of our experiences.
>
> —Thomas Jefferson

For an insurance agency:

> Life is all about options. Let us introduce you to yours.

For an exterminator:

> We'll take care of whatever is bugging you!

Back cover. Don't put much on the back cover. Do include your company name, address, telephone number, fax number, and website. If this is to be a mailer, leave space for a mailing label.

Inside flap. This is the key panel. Use it for glowing testimonials or for summarizing why the customer should choose you.

Inside three-panel spread. Keeping the reader in mind, discuss benefits.

- Detail your products, services, or processes.
- Include graphics, if relevant.
- State why you are the solution to the reader's problem(s).
- Support your claims.
- Share something of yourself and your company to set you apart from the competition.

Avoid overused expressions such as *the solution, user friendly, the best, one-stop shopping,* and so on. These seeds have been planted so many times they've mutated into weeds.

39

Remember that this is about your reader, not about you.

Too many people make the mistake of writing all about themselves. They include their mission statement and lots of sentences beginning "We can" or "We will." Remember that your reader doesn't care about you. Your reader wants to know the benefits of working with you or buying from you. (Refer specifically to No. 3 on your Start Up Sheet, "What's in it for my reader?")

Following is a brochure I use for my business writing workshop. Notice how I speak to the reader about benefits. (Check out Tip 126 for a discussion that differentiates features from benefits.)

Sample brochure (side 1)

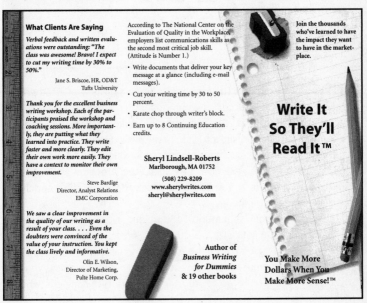

Sample brochure (side 2)

How much is poor writing costing you?

- If the **proposal** you wrote doesn't land the project you want, do you think the project went to an insider or to someone with a lower bid?

- If the **direct marketing** letter you sent doesn't yield the results you expect, do you blame it on a slumping market or on a list that wasn't targeted enough?

- If your **website** doesn't generate traffic, do you blame it on the viewer?

- If your **e-mail message** doesn't get results, do you blame it on the reader?

It's time you stopped blaming outside influences for the revenue and opportunities you're losing. Take control of your writing and have the impact you want to have in the marketplace.

Learn how to increase your bottom line significantly through superior writing skills.

Benefits of Attending

No matter what you write—letters, memos, e-mails, proposals, reports—this workshop is a must. In just one day you learn to create documents that drive action and affect your readers as you wish.

You bring to the workshop a document you need to write or rewrite, so you leave with a completed document (or a jump start on a long document). This is a tried-and-tested writing process you can apply immediately. Here are some of the hands-on experiences you can expect:

1. Getting Started (identify your reader and key issue)
2. Creating Dynamic Headlines
3. Writing the Draft
4. Designing for Visual Impact
5. Honing the Tone
6. Proofreading

Customized Workshops and Coaching: Workshops can be customized for specific groups such as executives, sales and marketing, technical and proposal writers, and others.

Selected Client List

- Baycare Health Partners
- Commonwealth of MA, Division of Health Care Finance & Policy
- EMC Corporation
- Financial Planners Association of Massachusetts
- International Data Group (IDG)
- Massachusetts Society of CPAs
- Tufts University
- U.S. Air Force (Hanscom AFB)

If you don't want the expense of hiring a graphic artist, there are many preprinted brochure blanks you can buy. One good source is PaperDirect. Get a catalog by calling 800-A-PAPER or checking out the website at http://www.paperdirect.com. In many cases, you can get matching stationery, envelopes, and business cards. The preceding example is a PaperDirect brochure blank. All I did was add the text. You can also check the large office-supply stores for brochure materials.

When you want something truly unique, work with a graphic designer. Look at lots of brochures and determine what you like. Then interview several graphic designers and ask to see samples of their work. Remember that price isn't the only criterion; this is your company's face to the world. You want to work with someone who can project your vision.

If you don't feel fully capable of writing the text yourself, work with a qualified writer who specializes in marketing. Just as with a graphic designer, ask to see writing samples, and don't base your decision on price alone.

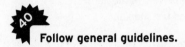

Follow general guidelines.

These guidelines will help you generate brochures that people read and keep, rather than use to line the bottom of their birdcages.

- **Keep the text short and simple.** Let the reader grasp the main points by simply glancing through the brochure.

- **Highlight your competitive advantage.** This is more important than providing long, boring descriptions of each of your products or services. Customers want to know why they should choose you over your competitors.

- **Use lots of headings and subheads.** This lets readers focus on parts that interest them.

- **Use bullets and/or numbers.** People don't read, they scan. Let them find important information quickly.

- **Avoid jargon and acronyms.** Use clear language everyone understands.

- **Refer readers to your website for more details.** If your brochure whets the reader's appetite, he will want to learn more.

When you include testimonials in your brochure, it's an immediate attestation to the quality of your product or service. Ask customers or clients whom you've delighted to supply testimonials. Most will be happy to help you but may not know what to write. You can help them by e-mailing a few questions or asking questions on the phone. Questions may include:

- Why did you select us?
- What was the best thing about working with us?
- Would you recommend us to others? Why or why not?

Once you get the customer's responses into a usable format, send a written copy for his approval. At the bottom of the quote, request formal permission to use his name and testimonial:

I give <name of business> permission to use this testimonial for marketing purposes.

_____   _____
Name   Date

Once you establish a look, feel, logo, and color scheme, use them for all your print and web material. This is called *branding*—creating your own image. You want to be recognizable and memorable.

If you fail to plan, you plan to fail.

UNKNOWN AUTHOR
(but often-used statement)

A business plan is essentially the road map to running your business. It incorporates what you hope to accomplish, how you intend to organize, and the resources you need to meet your goals. Here's what a business plan can do for you:

- Make you attractive to bankers or other funders
- Deal with problems before they happen or escalate
- Establish your vision and a strategy
- Determine timetables and budgets
- Create strategic alliances with other companies
- Provide employees with a vision for the company
- Convince suppliers and customers that you're a stable company with a promising future.

 Before you start writing your business plan, be certain you've gone through the process in Part One.

Determine what you need for content.

The length and content of your business plan is determined by the complexity of your business, your audience, and your purpose. If you want to attract bankers, venture capital investors, or angel investors, understand what they need to see. Contact several and ask about their expectations.

In addition to a title page and table of contents, your business plan may include (but is not limited to) the following:

Executive summary. Use the executive summary to capture the highlights of your business—it's the gateway to your entire plan. The executive summary must stand on its own and show passion. Use charts, tables, and graphs, when appropriate. (Check out Executive Summaries, beginning on page 83, for details.) At a minimum, include the following:

- Company's name and status
- Concrete and measurable goals and objectives
- Company description
- What's unique, special, or competitive about your product or service
- Market analysis (include your key competitors)
- Management team
- Financial analysis.

Mission statement. Include a mission statement to express the vision of your company. (For details, check out Mission Statements, beginning on page 115.)

Business description and concepts. This is the time to boast about how you started your business in your garage, how you grew your business, and where you plan to take the business. Provide a history of profits and anything else that toots your horn. Include charts, graphs, and tables.

Products and services. In jargon-free terms, help the reader to see, taste, smell, hear, and feel your product or service.

- How will it improve lives?
- What can you do better or more cost-effectively than others?
- Do you have a patent, or is one pending?

Market analysis and strategy. Show your solid understanding of the marketplace by discussing industry characteristics, trends, anticipated growth, complementary products or services, barriers of entry, and more.

Sales forecast. Make assumptions about sales (volume in units and dollars) for the coming year and for the next three to five years.

Marketing plan. Provide a marketing, advertising, and/or public relations plan. Indicate specific actions you plan to take, distribution channels, product and service warranties, tracking methods, and pricing. Start with the least expensive marketing tactics and proceed to the most expensive.

Operations plan. This is where you outline what's involved in operating this type of business. Include buildings, equipment, labor requirements, and all the bricks and mortar.

Financial plan. Include information about the company's financial status, new opportunities, strengths, weaknesses, opportunities for growth, ways to control costs, and more. If your company has established a history, provide sales forecasts, profit-and-loss statements, balance sheets, standard business ratios, and more.

Management team and key members. Don't underestimate the importance of collective genius. Describe your team's abilities, experiences, special skills, publications, patents, and anything else that shows strength. If someone on your team has had serious entrepreneurial success, you earn double points. Who wouldn't trust the business sense of Bill Gates or Steve Jobs?

Risk assessment. Include all the *what if*'s you can think of and how you plan to combat them.

Exit strategy. Present an exit strategy for you and/or your investors. (In X number of years you plan a merger, acquisition, initial purchase offering [IPO], or whatever.) This shows potential investors that you intend to strike it rich.

Appendices. Include resumes, promotional material, testimonials, product photos or sketches, lists of inventory and fixed assets, price lists, copies of legal agreements, articles about your product or service, and any other documents that add strength to your business plan.

- Have your lawyer, accountant, and trusted advisors review your business plan. They may find something you overlooked or underemphasized.

- Place your business plan in a three-ring binder. Don't get too fancy because you want to show that you're financially responsible.

- Review your business plan as needed. If your plan isn't working, review each section and make revisions. If economic conditions or your business model changes, update the plan.

If you're opening a restaurant or retail business, it's all about location, location, location. When your business plan is written to attract outside funders, be sure to include how you chose the location, why you chose the location, and what research pointed you to the location.

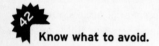

Know what to avoid.

Knowing what to avoid is as critical as knowing what to include. Avoid the following:

- **Waiting until the last minute.** This isn't like college where you can drink lots of coffee and cram all night. Your business plan must be well thought out. Take the time to do it right, and involve as many people as you need.

- **Worrying about being original.** Even an unoriginal idea can be propelled by a superior management team. Focus instead on finding highly capable people—people who may be able to attract investors and partners.

- **Being a windbag.** Try to keep your business plan to no more than 50 pages. Stick to the essential facts and stay focused.

- **Being a "big yawn" with dull formatting.** Jazz up your business plan with bullets, charts, numbers, tables, and a touch of color.

The name you select for your business will influence perceptions of customers, the media, joint venture partners, and others. For example, "Kabloom" is more original than "Metrowest Florist"; "Please Go Away Travel" is more creative than "FG&C Travel Agency." Here are some questions to ask when selecting a name for your business:

- How does the name sound?
- How long is the name?
- What personality does it convey?
- Is it vague and unspecific?
- Does it send a strong, positive message?
- Is there an association with an era, culture, or locale?

It's wise to stay away from initials because people tend to forget them or transpose them.

Our team is well balanced. We have problems everywhere.

TOMMY PROTHRO
American football coach

A *collaborative writing team* exists any time two or more people are involved in writing, editing, and/or approving a document—whether the document is for an internal or external audience. The team may be a writer and reviewer; a group of writers, editors, and one or more reviewers; or any combination of people with some level of responsibility in the overall project.

Before you start writing collaboratively, be certain you've gone through the process in Part One.

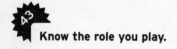

Know the role you play.

A team usually consists of some combination of the following: leader, delegator, writer, editor, and reviewer. And people often assume more than one role. For example, you may be a lead writer and delegate sections to other writers. Your role may differ from project to project or within a project. You may write one section, then be asked to edit someone else's section.

All team members should have a clear understanding of their roles and the pecking order. Although this sounds basic, it's often the area where people trip over each other. Some people enjoy being part of a collaborative team; others don't. If you don't, try to view the experience as an opportunity to benefit from the wisdom and talents of others.

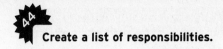

Create a list of responsibilities.

You need a list that identifies the tasks, leaders, responsibilities, and procedures. Feel free to pick and choose from the sample checklist that follows to create a list that works for your project. After the team agrees to each member's responsibilities, everyone should sign the agreement and receive a copy.

WHO'S-DOING-WHAT CHECKLIST

Team Leader

Who is responsible for keeping the team on task, leading meetings, and coordinating communication?

Team Responsibilities

- What specific tasks must be completed to finish the project?
- Who is responsible for each task?

Working Procedures

- When, where, and how often will the team meet?
- What procedures will be followed in the meetings?
- How will decisions be made, by majority or consensus?
- How will team members communicate—by e-mail? by phone? face to face?

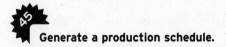

Generate a production schedule.

Team members don't always realize the impact of missing a deadline, and you may have to stress the importance of observing schedules. Ideally, your production schedule (or milestone chart) builds in extra time for unexpected delays. Make sure it includes columns for both the date targeted and the date completed. Also, understand which steps can be done concurrently. Following is an example of a production schedule. Make your own to identify your milestones.

PRODUCTION SCHEDULE <Name of Project>			
Milestone	**Target Date**	**Actual Date**	**Person Responsible**
Fill out Start Up Sheet			
Brainstorming Session			
First Draft Delivered			
Visuals Prepared			
Comments Due			
Final Draft Submitted			
Final Visuals Submitted			
Final Draft Approved			
Final Visuals Approved			
Print			
Deliverable/Available Date			

Fill out the Start Up Sheet in Part One when the entire team is assembled so you have everyone's participation. Too often the people responsible for signing off don't get involved until the end. If everyone isn't on the same page from the beginning, the results can be disastrous. If you can't assemble the entire team, fill out the Start Up Sheet with as many people as you can round up. Before going further, get written approval from those who aren't present.

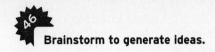

46 Brainstorm to generate ideas.

Brainstorming is a great getting-started strategy for collaborative writing. It moves ideas from people's heads to paper, and offers an opportunity for the entire team to give and get input on content and structure. If you can't assemble the entire team, get written approval for the outline from those who weren't there before you go further. Here are some brainstorming tips followed by a sample brainstorming exercise:

- Don't pass judgment; every idea is worth hearing.
- Don't dwell on any one idea.
- Make a diagram with a circle in the center that states your purpose.
- Use branches and limbs to extend ideas, as in the example below.

Brainstorming exercise

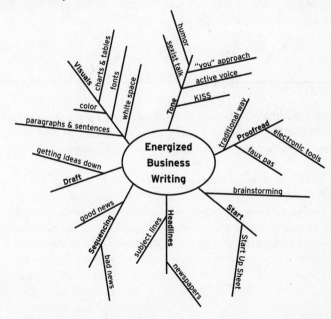

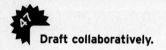

Draft collaboratively.

If more than one person is doing the writing, break the project into manageable chunks and assign sections accordingly. Each writer can draft a chapter, section, or whatever makes sense. Ultimately the document must sound as if one person wrote it. That's generally the job for a good editor—if you have the luxury of one.

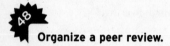

Organize a peer review.

For a large project, a peer review is appropriate after the first draft is complete. It's the time to get everyone's input on general content, formatting, and any other issues that may haunt you later. If you can't assemble everyone, gather as many people as you can.

Use group writing tools.

Mark up text without destroying the original. There are many tools to use that including split screens and tracking. Keep in mind that even though reviewers make comments, the author owns the final copy.

> Two heads may be better than one, but two egos are worse. Typically, everyone who reviews a document feels compelled to comment. That's just human nature. It isn't necessarily a reflection on your writing or your style; it's just part of the process. Never take this personally.

*Half the battle in communicating effectively by e-mail
is getting the other party just to open your message. In a
spam-filled world, the ability to craft a compelling
subject line is an art—not a science.*

MARK VEREKA, *Barron's*

E-mail has done for writing what the telephone has done for the voice. An e-mail can reach your reader in a matter of seconds, whether you send it across the building or across the globe. It's often the first (and only) impression your reader has of you. What do you want that impression to be?

 Before you start writing an e-mail, be certain you've gone through the process in Part One.

50

Write a subject line that delivers an informative, compelling message.

The subject line is the most important piece of information in an e-mail message. It stands alone to pull in your audience without the benefit of context. Your words are trapped inside a field with competing subject lines, unable to set themselves apart with bold, italics, or underscore.

There are people who get hundreds of e-mail messages a day, and they can't possibly read them all. So if your subject line doesn't seduce the reader, he may never open your message. If you look down the subject line column of your inbox, perhaps you see subject lines such as these that give you absolutely no information and no reason to check the message:

One more thing. . .
Friday
Follow-up
Please do me a favor
Meeting

On the front page of *USA Today* is a column called "Newsline" that offers informative headlines on what's happening around the world. You can read the headlines and get a snapshot of major stories. Think of how informative it would be to read the subject column of your inbox and get that same level of information.

Always include in your subject line a key piece of information so your reader can get the gist of your message at a glance. Observe the following sets of subject lines and how much more the *Informative*'s tell you.

Informative:	15% profit expected for Q2
Uninformative:	Profit report
Informative:	MIS: Urgent meeting 5/6 @ 2:15 in Blue Rm
Uninformative:	MIS Meeting
Informative:	Brad Jones joining Mktg. Grp. 9/10
Uninformative:	New hire
Informative:	Contact is Jane Brown at Mellows Co.
Uninformative:	Contact

When you abbreviate, be certain the reader will understand your abbreviation. For example, in the United States, we recognize 5/6 as May 6. In Europe or in the military, 5/6 is June 5.

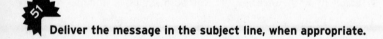

Deliver the message in the subject line, when appropriate.

When you can, deliver your message as the subject line and don't write in the text box. Put your initials at the end of the message, and your reader knows that the subject line is the message.

Following is a series of e-mail subject lines I exchanged with a colleague. We rescheduled a meeting, and neither of us ever wrote in the text box. Usually I don't recommend scheduling appointments via e-mail because it's more efficient to schedule appointments when you're both looking at your calendars. However, I know my audience. This woman lives and breathes e-mail and doesn't return phone calls.

> Mon. doesn't work. How's Tues? —SLR
> Tues is NG. How's Wed? —MN
> Wed. is fine. —SLR
> See you Wed. at 3:15. —MN

When you first start sending subject lines without a text box, most people will get it right away and respond in the same manner. A few, however, will let you know that they "didn't get your message." When you tell them you try to save them time by delivering the message in the subject line when you can, they too will start using this electronic shorthand.

Instead of your initials, you may use —END or —EOM (end of message). For example, you may write the following subject line and not put anything in the text box. After all, what else is there to say?

> I'll finish the report Friday morning.—EOM

I don't recommend this type of electronic shorthand when you write to someone you don't know because they may view it as slightly curt. It's for colleagues with whom you communicate regularly. However, you should always use a descriptive subject line.

52 Change the subject line when replying to a message.

When you reply to someone's message, change the subject line. To maintain continuity in a stream of messages, keep the key word in the subject line and add the change to the message. For example: "Billing: To be discussed at April mtg."

My colleague, James, tells the story of coming to work one foggy morning and noticing a parked car with its lights on. He sent an e-mail to the entire distribution list with this subject line: "Lic. #234 ADB car lights on." Realizing that James was in the office, people took the opportunity to send him their own messages. One person asked James to meet her for lunch; another wanted to find out when a seminar was being offered; and another wanted some other information. None of the people changed the subject line from "Lic. #234 ADB car lights on," although none of the messages had anything to do with the one James sent.

53 Know when to reply to sender or to all.

When you reply to a message, ask yourself who needs your reply—everyone or the sender?

A colleague sent a notice to her distribution list of 10 business friends letting everyone know that her mother had died. Of the 10 who received the message, 8 sent e-mail condolences by replying to all. Only the sender should have received the condolences. *Replying to all isn't the only thing wrong here.* When you send condolences to someone, don't do it through e-mail. This is a perfect example of where a handwritten note of sympathy or a card is more appropriate.

54 Use a salutation and a complimentary closing.

Would you start a telephone call without saying hello or end without saying goodbye? Of course not. Would you send a letter without a salutation or a complimentary closing? Of course not. Apply the same courtesies to e-mail. Start each e-mail message with a salutation and end with a closing. Unlike the formal salutations and closings in letters, e-mail salutations and closings are less formal. Here are a few examples:

Salutations	Closings
Hi Ken,	Regards,
Hello everyone,	See you later,
Hi,	Best wishes,
Ken,	Thanks,

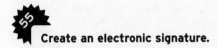

Create an electronic signature.

Prepare an electronic signature file that ends each message. (Check your software for assistance if you don't know how.) This gives contact information—like letterhead on stationery. It also creates free advertising on every message you send. In addition to your name and title, consider including your e-mail address, website, phone number, and some information about your business:

Alan Wright
Wright Brothers Financial Advisors
alan@wrightbrothers.com
www.wrightbrothers.com
212-555-0000

When you quit working, make sure your money doesn't.

Click here to learn about our retirement seminar on March 3.

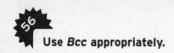

56

Use *Bcc* appropriately.

Bcc means "blind copy." It's for situations when you don't want the addressee to know you're sending a copy to a third party. Use *Bcc* prudently because it's a clear indication you're sending something unbeknownst to the person or people in the *To* field.

Have you ever received an impersonal e-mail, such as the one that follows, with your name and many others in the *To* field or *Cc* field?

To:	jondoe@aol.com; Allison@earthlink.net; grace_powell @waters.com; gbassill@globaltechnology.com; ed_smith@comcast.net; bmt@aol.com; Frank_stein@ frankensteindustries.com; Pollyanna@goldmac.com

Here's how to avoid that: When you send an e-mail message to groups of people, place their e-mail addresses in the *Bcc* field. The people whose addresses are typed in the *Bcc* field get a copy of the message, but they don't see the names of the other *Bcc* recipients. The outgoing *Bcc* looks like this:

Bcc:	jondoe@aol.com; Allison@earthlink.net; grace_powell@ waters.com; gbassill@globaltechnology.com; ed_smith@comcast.net; bmt@aol.com; Frank_stein@ frankensteindustries.com; Pollyanna@goldmac.com

But when jondoe receives the message in his inbox, only his name appears in the *To* field:

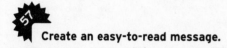

57

Create an easy-to-read message.

When you send someone a let's-do-lunch message, of course you don't need to write a draft. Otherwise, it's critical that you do.

Include the who, what, when, where, why, *and* how *in the first paragraph.* Lots of people read e-mails on hand-held computers where the screen displays only a small amount of information. Therefore, it's imperative that you answer the questions the reader will have—and do it in the first paragraph. Check out Tip 11 for more information on anticipating the right questions.

Create visual impact. What you learned in Visual Impact, beginning on page 21, applies to e-mails. All too often we get messages where a paragraph goes on for one or more screens. Here are some ways to give your e-mail visual appeal:

- Use headlines and subheads.
- Use bulleted and numbered lists, when appropriate.
- Limit paragraphs to eight lines of text.
- Double-space between paragraphs.
- NEVER USE ALL CAPS.
- Use correct grammar and punctuation.

Remember that e-mail is a serious business document. Treat e-mail with the same respect as any other business document you write. At first glance, the following *Before* e-mail may seem fine. However, when you look at the *After*, you notice the difference.

Before: What's wrong?

- The subject line gives no valuable information.
- There's no salutation or closing.
- Nothing stands out.
- The text is wordy.

E-mail (Before)

To:	**Distribution List**
Subject:	**Merger**

Rumors have been flying about the possibility of merging with Ken-San Company. Well, let me give you the facts. As of January 1 we'll become a wholly owned subsidiary of Ken-San Company. We've worked hard for this and know it comes as good news. There are two key advantages. This is what they are: We'll have added strength in terms of public acceptance and operating capital and we'll be able to serve our customers more promptly, efficiently, and thoroughly. This is something every company should strive for because customers are the backbone of any business. We are sure you have a lot of questions, and we want to be sure that you have a chance to air them. We'll be sponsoring a company-wide buffet luncheon, which will give you a chance to have all your questions answered. Barbara N. Arthur from the Ken-San Company will be on hand to answer your questions.

I'm sure many of you are wondering about the future of your jobs. Ms. Arthur will be letting you know firsthand of the company's sincere intentions to continue operating this division autonomously. Here are the details of the luncheon: Everyone must attend. The luncheon will be at the Apollo Restaurant on July 15. It will start at noon and will run until 1:30. We look forward to seeing you there.

After: What's right?

- The subject line tells the story as in a newspaper headline.
- There's a salutation and a closing.
- Key information stands out with headlines and bullets.
- Readers can scan the message and get key information at a glance.
- There are fewer words.
- There's more white space.

E-mail (After)

To:	Distribution List
Subject:	**Yes, we're merging with Ken-San Company**

Dear Colleagues,

Yes, We're Merging
We start the new year as a wholly owned subsidiary of Ken-San Company.

Key Advantages: Operating Capital & Customer Satisfaction
- We'll have added strength in terms of public acceptance and operating capital.
- We'll be able to serve our customers more promptly, efficiently, and thoroughly.

Learn More Over Lunch
We'll be sponsoring a company-wide buffet luncheon. Representatives of Ken-San will be on hand to answer any questions. <u>Attendance is mandatory</u>.

When:	July 15, 12:00–1:30
Where:	Apollo Restaurant

Regards,
Bill

If your message is more than two screens, think about sending it as an attachment. You may consider including in the text box a very brief summary of the longer message. Also consider sending an attachment if the message is heavily formatted. In that way you can be reasonably sure your reader will see your message as you intend it to be seen.

Instant-messaging shortcuts (LOL for "laughing out loud," for example) are fine if you're a teenager writing to your friends. They're not appropriate in business. Neither are the little emoticons. :-}

*A recent government publication on the marketing
of cabbage contains, according to one report,
26,941 words. It is noteworthy in this regard that
the Gettysburg Address contains a mere 279 words
while the Lord's Prayer comprises but 67.*

NORMAN R. AUGUSTINE
American author and former chairman,
Martin Marietta Corporation

The purpose of an executive summary is to consolidate the key points of a document in one place. It's intended for the busy executive who may use the information to make personnel, funding, policy, or other decisions based on what they read in this condensed version.

In *Effective Communications for Engineers*, author Roy B. Hughson cites a study done by Westinghouse Electric Corporation entitled "How Managers Read Reports." The study confirms that managers read executive summaries even though they may read little else. Here are the main parts of a report and the percentage of managers who read them:

- Executive summary: 100 percent
- Introduction: 65 percent
- Body: 22 percent
- Conclusions: 55 percent
- Appendix: 15 percent

Before you start writing your executive summary, be certain you've gone through the process in Part One.

58

Write the executive summary after you finish the longer document.

You write an executive summary after you write the document—so don't even try to do it before. (Think about it. You can't write a book report before you read the book.) Keep in mind that high-level executives need high-level information. That's the reason a very small percentage of executives read the body or the appendix.

Here's how to begin writing an executive summary that's meaningful:

- Scan the overall document to determine the content, structure, and length.
- Review your research to determine the keys ideas and concepts.
- Group ideas logically.
- Outline the key elements and the minor points that support them.
- Include findings or conclusions.
- Use graphics that make a strong statement.

 Here are some guidelines for determining length:

If the document is . . .	write a summary of . . .
up to 50 pages	1 or 2 pages
51 to 100 pages	2 or 3 pages
more than 100 pages	3 or 4 pages

59

Use technical terms cautiously.

Use technical terms only when you're sure the executives reading the report are familiar with them. Not all executives have technical backgrounds, so err on the side of being conservative or offering explanations. For example, if you're using initialisms or acronyms, spell them out and follow with the abbreviated form:

- light amplification by stimulated emission of radiation (laser)
- Performance Evaluation and Review Technique (PERT)

When you need to attract investors to your business, include an executive summary as the first section of your business plan. (Check out Business Plans, beginning on page 63.)

60 Sequence information to have the most impact on your reader.

In Tip 13 you learned about sequencing your information for maximum impact. For an executive who will be responsive, pleased, or neutral, put the key issue at the beginning of the executive summary. For an executive who will be unresponsive or disappointed, put the key issue at the end, so you can build up to it. Because the executive summary may be the basis for major decisions, sequencing is critical. Check out the *Before* and *After* examples that follow. They're written for a neutral reader.

Before: This document is sequenced Background, Approach, Findings. By addressing the Background and Approach first, you build up to the Findings the executive may not view as good news. This sequencing is appropriate when the reader will be unresponsive or disappointed, but here the reader is neutral.

Executive summary for a neutral reader (Before)

Background
This study documents the costs and benefits of potential US Coast Guard Vessel Traffic Services (VTS) in selecting US deep-draft ports on the Atlantic, Gulf, and Pacific coasts. The concept of VTS has gained international acceptance by governments and

maritime industries as a means of advancing safety in rapidly expanding ports and waterways. VTS communications are advisory in nature, providing timely and accurate information to mariners, thereby enhancing the potential for avoiding vessel casualties. This study builds on the experience of earlier efforts and provides the most comprehensive and quantitative analyses of VTS costs and benefits.

Approach

The following summarizes the seven steps used to gather the data:

- Defining study zones and subzones.
- Analyzing historical vessel casualties.
- Forecasting avoidable future vessel casualties in each study zone.
- Estimating the avoidable consequences in each study zone, the associated physical losses, and the dollar values of these avoidable losses.
- Estimating the costs of a state-of-the-art Candidate VTS Design for each study zone.
- Comparing the benefits and costs among the 22 zones.
- Analyzing the sensitivity of relative net benefits among study zones to a range of uncertainty in key input variables.

Findings

The study indicates that the 22 study zones can be divided into three groups in terms of their relative life-cycle net benefits. The following groupings are divided into areas of sensitivity: The net benefit is positive in New Orleans, Port Arthur, Houston/Galveston, Mobile, Los Angeles/Long Beach, Corpus Christi. It is sensitive in New York, Tampa, Portland (Oregon), Philadelphia/Delaware Bay, Chesapeake North/Baltimore, Providence, Long Island Sound, Puget Sound. And it's negative in Jacksonville, Wilmington, Santa Barbara, Portsmouth, Portland (Maine), San Francisco, Anchorage/Cook Inlet, Chesapeake South/Hampton Roads.

After: This document is sequenced Findings, Approach, Background. Since the reader in question is neutral, why make him search for the one piece of information he needs? In addition,

- Headlines are self-explanatory, giving information at a glance.
- Key information stands out because it is presented as a table.
- The list is numbered, rather than bulleted, to show the order of steps.

Executive summary for a neutral reader (After)

This study documents the costs and benefits of potential US Coast Guard Vessel Traffic Services (VTS) in selecting US deep-draft ports on the Atlantic, Gulf, and Pacific coasts.

Findings: Zones can be divided into three groups
The study indicates that the 22 study zones can be divided into three groups according to the sensitivity of relative net benefits:

Sensitivity	Ports
Positive	New Orleans, Port Arthur, Houston/Galveston, Mobile, Los Angeles/Long Beach, Corpus Christi
Sensitive	New York, Tampa, Portland (Oregon), Philadelphia/Delaware Bay, Chesapeake North/Baltimore, Providence, Long Island Sound, Puget Sound
Negative	Jacksonville, Wilmington, Santa Barbara, Portsmouth, Portland (Maine), San Francisco, Anchorage/Cook Inlet, Chesapeake South/Hampton Roads

Approach: Seven steps used to gather data

The following summarizes the seven steps used to gather the data:

1. Defining study zones and subzones.
2. Analyzing historical vessel casualties.
3. Forecasting avoidable future vessel casualties in each study zone.
4. Estimating the avoidable consequences in each study zone, the associated physical losses, and the dollar values of these avoidable losses.
5. Estimating the costs of a state-of-the-art Candidate VTS Design for each study zone.
6. Comparing the benefits and costs among the 22 zones.
7. Analyzing the sensitivity of relative net benefits among study zones to a range of uncertainty in key input variables.

Background

The concept of VTS has gained international acceptance by governments and maritime industries to advance safety in rapidly expanding ports and waterways. VTS communications provide timely and accurate information to mariners, thereby enhancing the potential for avoiding vessel casualties. This study builds on the experience of earlier efforts and provides the most comprehensive and quantitative analyses of VTS costs and benefits.

They laughed at Columbus, they laughed at Fulton, they laughed at the Wright Brothers. But they also laughed at Bozo the Clown.

CARL SAGAN
Astronomer

Grant money provides research groups and the nonprofit sector with funding for worthwhile projects. Funders are practically waiting in line to finance promising ideas. Grants are issued by federal and state agencies, community foundations, corporations, international organizations, and other groups.

A grant proposal should be based on the belief that a partnership between the soliciting organization and the funder will result in a dynamic collaboration. When applying for a grant, show the intended funder that with the necessary dollars you can solve a specific problem or need.

Before you start writing your grant, be certain you've gone through the process in Part One. Fill out the Start Up Sheet for Grant Writing in this section rather than the generic one.

START UP SHEET FOR GRANT WRITING

1. Does this overlap another grant (internal, perhaps)? If so, what makes my request different?

2. What are my specific needs? (Remember to follow the needs, not the money.)

3. What's my goal? (State in one sentence.)

---

4. What are my objectives, short- and long-term?

5. How will I measure success?

6. What are my budgetary needs?

7. What's the timeline?

8. What's the sustainability?

9. What are my plans for promoting the program?

10. Who is my target population?

11. What are the best practices?

12. Who is my reader?

13. Is anyone else working on another aspect of this proposal?

14. Why is my organization more qualified than others to do
_____?

15. What's the one key point I want my readers to remember?

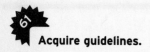

Acquire guidelines.

Request guidelines from the potential funder and read them very carefully. Guidelines tell you about deadlines, eligibility, format, timetable,
budgets, funding goals and priorities, award levels, the evaluation process
and criteria, contact information, and other submission requirements.

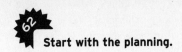

Start with the planning.

Successful grant writing involves the coordination of several activities: planning, searching for data and resources, writing and packaging the grant, submitting the grant, and following up. It's critical to put the time into planning in order to reap the rewards. Here are some planning tips:

- Define your project.
- Clarify its purpose with a mission statement.
- Define the scope of work.
- Determine the goals and objectives.

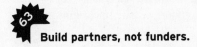

Build partners, not funders.

When you write a grant and treat the intended funder as a partner, you have a much better chance of accomplishing your goal. Ask yourself these questions:

- **What is the need or problem?** Cast the question in terms of the need for the greater good, not your need.

- **Who else is addressing this need or problem?** Identify areas where help is still needed.

- **How do I propose addressing the need or problem?** Paint a picture so your prospect sees your plan in action.

- **How will my plan solve the need or problem?** State what will be different or improved when the project is completed.

- **How will I know that I'm successful?** Include the measurements you'll use to determine success.

- **What resources do I already have?** Give information about your resources—both paid and volunteer.

- **What are my qualifications?** List your experience, key accomplishments, past successes, and anything else showing you're the one who can solve this need or problem.

- **What problems or barriers do I foresee?** Demonstrate that this project is well thought through by discussing any roadblocks you anticipate and how you plan to overcome them.

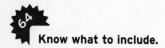

Know what to include.

The extent of information you include is relative to how large the project is and how much money you request. Following is a detailed list of the parts of a typical grant. Yours may have more or fewer inclusions.

Transmittal letter. Send a one-page cover letter on your letterhead. Include in the first paragraph the reason for your application and the amount of your request.

Title page. Include the title of the project; the name, address, and telephone number of the project director; the name of the group or individual requesting the grant; and the project's beginning and end date.

Table of contents. If the proposal is more than 10 pages long, include a table of contents so potential funders can find key information quickly.

Executive summary. Nearly 90 percent of all funding decisions are made before the potential funder finishes this section. (Check out Executive Summaries, beginning on page 83, for details on making your executive summary clear, concise, and effective.)

Introduction. In one page, introduce the following:

- **Concept.** Explain how this project fits into the philosophy and mission of your organization.

- **Key elements of the program.** Include the nature of the project, a timetable, anticipated outcomes, and staffing needs.
- **Overview of the financials.** At this stage you may not be able to pinpoint all expenses, but you can present broad outlines.

Goals and objectives. Express your goal—the end result—in a powerful sentence. Support your goal with the long- and short-term objectives, which are the steps along the way. Include the following:

- Measurable milestones you will reach in meeting those goals and objectives
- How you will know that you're making progress towards your goals and objectives.

Budgetary needs. You probably won't be able to pin down all the expenses until the details and timing are finalized. For the purpose of writing the grant, sketch out the broad outlines of the budget to be sure the costs are in proportion to the outcomes you anticipate. If it appears that the costs will be prohibitive, scale back your plans or adjust them to remove expenses that aren't cost effective. Also, mention funding from other sources, volunteer services, and the like.

Timeline. State how long this project should take and the steps along the way. Present the timeline in a graphical format to make it easy to read.

Sustainability. If the program is proving to be successful and funding runs out, would you seek alternative sources of funding? Detail the following:

- How the program can run on its own
- Whether you would seek funding from other resources
- Whether you'd seek additional funding from this funder.

Promotion. Outline your plans for promoting the program. Will you use a public relations campaign? Community affairs organizations? Professional journals?

Target population. If your target population is a factor, detail who they are. For example, an organization doing research on a specific disease may do a study whose target population is a certain ethnic group of certain ages.

Best practices. How will you share the success of your project with other organizations or communities? Will you share the "lessons learned" so others can benefit from what worked and what didn't work? What lessons learned from others will you include?

Qualifications. Many groups are vying for the same dollars. Detail why you're more qualified or better able to reach your goal.

- If you've had a breakthrough or success on something similar in the past, be specific about how you met your goals.
- Percentages and dollar amounts can be powerful.
- If you have key people who will lead the charge, include their resumes.

Appendices. Place resumes and any supporting documentation in the appendices.

Glossary. Throughout the grant, keep industry-specific terms, acronyms, or initialisms to a minimum. When you do need to include them, use a glossary for easy reference.

 Describe your program with facts, statistics, and passion using action-packed words such as

- achieve
- cooperative
- enhancing
- establish
- existing
- expanding
- overall
- strategies.

Present your goals in visionary terms and your objectives in measurable terms with performance words such as

- decrease
- deliver
- develop
- establish
- improve
- increase
- produce.

Don't beat around the bush about future funding. Use phrases such as

- creating future fundraising partners
- inviting more external funding sources
- local fundraising
- seeking to identify more stakeholders.

Use high-quality paper that doesn't appear to be too expensive. You don't want to be viewed as a big spender or you weaken your chances of getting the funding. Consider using recycled paper.

If your funding request is denied, request feedback about your proposal's strengths and weaknesses. This information isn't always forthcoming. When it is, however, it can be invaluable for future submissions.

*Why is there never enough time to do a job right,
but always enough time to do it over?*

ANONYMOUS

The reality of writing instructions and procedures is that no one really wants to read them. People want products and processes that are simple and intuitive. They typically refer to instructions and procedures when they have problems or need to figure out difficult steps.

For example, when you buy a car, you already know how to unlock it, start it, honk the horn, and fasten your seat belt. Those things are simple and intuitive. What's not simple and intuitive is knowing how to use the neat radio/tape-recorder/CD/equalizer unit with its 10-speaker stereo and 40 buttons. That's when you may need to read the instructions. You improve the odds of your instructions being read when you make them clear and simple.

 Before you start writing your instructions or procedures, be certain you've gone through the process in Part One.

65

Think of yourself as the teacher and the reader as the learner.

When writing instructions or procedures, it is especially important to remember your audience, as mentioned in Tip 2. An artist may process information differently from an engineer. Consider these guidelines:

Audience	Personality Type	Best Presentation
academic, scientific, or technical	process-oriented	step-by-step instructions
business or law	answer-oriented	quick answers
creative	visually oriented	drawings, charts, tables, flow charts, illustrations, photographs

66 Understand how your reader will use the instructions.

Should you deliver your instructions on paper, a CD-ROM, the Web, or a combination? The following may help you to decide:

■ People who need to install equipment on a shop floor may not have a computer. For them you write a paper-based manual.

■ People who are computer literate and have access to computers benefit from a CD-ROM or Web-based instructions. The advantage to Web-based instructions is that they can be updated as necessary.

■ State all the information the reader needs to know at the beginning of the instructions or procedures. For example, does the task require special materials or tools? If so, start with "Tools Required" or "Materials Required."

■ If there are any dangerous steps or any cautions the reader should know about, use labels such as "Danger" or "Caution." (Check out Tip 70.)

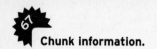

Chunk information.

Organize information into manageable chunks. Then break the chunks into separate sections, chapters, or subchapters. For example, if writing instructions for word-processing software, identify the tasks commonly performed by users, then break them into categories.

- **Writing:** Compose, save, edit, cut, copy, paste.
- **Printing:** Whole documents, individual pages, selections.
- **Graphics:** Charts, tables, lists, text alignment.

Use parallel structure for headings, subheadings, and lists. In the following *Not Parallel* list, the word *how* stands out like a wart on the end of someone's nose because every other line begins with a verb ending in *-ing*.

Parallel	Not Parallel
Accessing the program	Accessing the program
Changing your password	Changing your password
Entering information	How to enter information
Exiting the program	Exiting the program

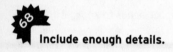

Include enough details.

You must write instructions with clarity and keen attention to detail. Never assume your reader will read between the lines or read your mind.

- **Be precise about locations such as top, bottom, left, and right.** Locations are subjective. "The switch is on the left" depends on which way the reader faces. Instead say, "As you face the front of the room, the switch is on the left."

- **Use *clockwise* and *counterclockwise* to describe turns.** "Rotate the dial 45 degrees to create a seal" doesn't tell the reader which way to turn the dial. When you say "Rotate the dial 45 degrees clockwise to create a seal," the direction is clear.

 Do not assume prior knowledge on the part of your reader. What is obvious to you may not be obvious to him. Try to complete the exercise below. Are the instructions fully and clearly expressed?

The following figure shows nine dots. Join them together using four straight lines *without lifting your pencil from the paper*. (For help, see page 102.)

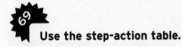

Use the step-action table.

With a step-action table, instructions and procedures are easy to write and easy to read. To make one, create two columns. Label the first column "Step" and the second column "Action."

- Each step should tell the reader to do something.

- Each action should start with an active verb.

  Active: Press the <whatever> key.
  Passive: The <whatever> key should be pressed.

  Active: Sign the vacation request.
  Passive: The vacation request must be signed by the employee.

- In each action box, you can include results, notes, diagrams, screen shots, *what if*'s, or other relevant details.

Before: What's wrong?

- The steps don't start with action words.
- Steps identified as 3 and 4 aren't steps; they're notes for Step 2.
- Step 5 combines the action with notes about the action.

Procedure table (Before)

Step	Action
1	All records must be signed in black or blue ink.
2	All mistakes must be corrected with a single line through the mistake, initialed, and dated with the correct date.
3	No whiteout or correction tape is allowed.
4	No backdating is allowed.
5	All incidents of lost documentation must be reported to the Documentation Supervisor. For a lost controlled document, the Documentation Supervisor will make a note of the incident in the controlled distribution record and will issue a replacement document. For a lost quality record, a memo will be placed in the appropriate file.

After: What's right?

- Each step starts with an action word.
- Notes are set apart and organized with bullets.

Procedure table (After)

Step	Action
1	Sign all records in black or blue ink.

2	Correct all mistakes with a single line through the mistake, then initial and date with the correct date.
	Notes:
	• You can't use whiteout or correction tape.
	• You can't backdate.
3	Report all incidents of lost documentation to the Documentation Supervisor.
	Notes:
	• For a lost controlled document, the Documentation Supervisor will make a note of the incident in the controlled distribution record and will issue a replacement document.
	• For a lost quality record, a memo will be placed in the appropriate file.

Highlight warnings.

You are not only responsible for telling your readers what they *should* do, you must also tell them what they *shouldn't* do. When performing a certain task may lead to something dangerous (electric shock, erasing a disk drive, toxic fumes, equipment damage, baldness, and the like), you must clearly highlight the danger. Use the word *Warning* or an icon:

 Airborne particles of respirable size of crystalline silica are known to cause cancer. They must be buried in approved land disposal facilities in accordance with federal, state, and local regulations.

Test, test, and test again.

You won't know whether your instructions or procedures are easy to understand until you test them extensively.

Years ago, I wrote a user manual for a company that developed accounting software. I asked a novice to test what I wrote. When the novice was instructed to press a numeric key, his fingers headed straight for the numerals on top of the alpha keyboard. He couldn't get the numbers to show up on the computer screen. The problem? I was accustomed to using the numeric keypad and neglected to mention that users needed to use this keypad, not the "typewriter" numeric keys. The moral of the story is don't take anything for granted. Test, test, and test again.

Here are some suggestions for testing:

- Ask a novice user to read the instructions to make sure that they are accurate and easily understood. A novice often finds a need for explanations you take for granted.

- Ask a person who represents the ability of the intended user to see if she can easily understand the instructions.

- Ask an expert in the technical area of the subject to review the instructions for accuracy. This is often referred to as a technical edit.

- Test the instructions in typical user environments, if possible.

ANSWER TO THE PUZZLE IN TIP 68

If you couldn't join the nine dots together with four straight lines without lifting your pencil, it's because the instructions were vague. If they were detailed, they would have told you where to start and that you don't need to stay within the parameters of the square. Here's the solution:

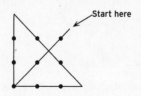

Start here

*Writing good letters—communicating on the
deeper level of thoughts, feelings, and ideas rather
than on the shallow, superficial level of events—affects
our ability to think clearly, to reason accurately,
and to be understood effectively.*

STEPHEN R. COVEY
The 7 Habits of Highly Effective People

Letter-writing is of noble ancestry, going back over 4,000 years in the ancient Near East. The kings of Egypt, for example, wrote letters to their vassal princes on moist clay tablets. The tablets were then baked and sent to the recipient by messenger. Because hard clay tablets were heavy, brevity and conciseness were important for letter-writing even then. If the king's letters had taken up too many tablets, the messengers would have collapsed from exhaustion.

Of course, methods have changed dramatically from the demise of the clay tablet, the quill pen, and the manual typewriter. But one thing hasn't changed—the need to get your point across clearly and concisely. If your messages aren't concise, postal workers will collapse under the weight of your letters.

Before you start writing your letter, be certain you've gone through the process in Part One.

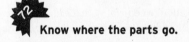

Know where the parts go.

Following are all the parts that can be included in a letter and the order in which they appear. It's doubtful that you'd use every part in every letter, so this is for placement only. Check out pages 110–111 for a sample letter.

Dateline: Open every letter with a date. Remember that people in Europe and in the military put the day before the month: 7 May 20—.

Mailing or in-house notations: Place mailing notations (special delivery, certified mail, registered mail, air mail, by messenger) or in-house notations (personal, confidential) two lines below the date. Type them in all capital letters.

Inside address: Start the inside address four lines below the dateline. If you use a mailing or in-house notation, start the inside address two lines below the notation. The inside address contains everything you need to deliver the letter: name, job title, street address or post office box number, suite or room number, city, state, and Zip Code.

 http://www.usps.com/ncsc/lookups/usps_abbreviations.html has a complete listing of state and territory abbreviations, street suffixes, and secondary unit designators.

Salutation: Place the salutation two lines below the address. The salutation should correspond directly to the first line of the inside address. For example, if your addressees are Dr. and Mrs. Eric Lindsell, the salutation should read "Dear Dr. and Mrs. Lindsell." If you write to a company and don't know the addressee's name (and can't find it out), you may substitute his job title in the salutation ("Dear Public Relations Director," for example).

- In most cases, place a colon after the salutation.
- Place a comma after the salutation when you are calling the addressee by his first name. Use the addressee's first name only if you know him well.

Subject line: Place the subject line two lines below the salutation; it's part of the body, not the heading. The subject line describes the purpose of the letter.

Body (message): The body supports the theme of the message. Single-space the body of the letter, and double-space between paragraphs. Double-space the body only when the message is just a few sentences.

Complimentary closing: Place the complimentary closing two lines below the last line of the body. Capitalize only the first word, and place a comma after the last word.

Signature block: Present the signature block in any of the following ways. Leave enough room to sign your name.

Very truly yours,

Steven Albert

Steven Albert

Very truly yours,

Steven Albert

Steven Albert, President

Very truly yours,

S.E.A. Construction, Inc.

Steven Albert

Steven Albert, President

Very truly yours,

Steven Albert

Steven Albert

President

Reference initials: Use reference initials to identify the author of the letter and/or the typist. Type them at the left margin, two lines below the signature line. When you write your own letter, don't use initials.

Enclosure notation: When you enclose anything in the envelope besides the letter, place an enclosure notation on the line directly below the reference initials. In some offices, when something is attached rather than enclosed, the word *Attachment* will appear in place of *Enclosure*. You can use any of the following styles:

Enclosure

Enc.

Encls.

l Attachment

1 Enc.

Attachments: 2

Enc. (2)

Enclosures:

    1. Purchase Order No. 3434

    2. Check No. 567

Copy notation: When you send a copy of the letter to a third person, place a notation to that effect directly below the enclosure notation or reference initials. The *cc* notation is a holdover from the days of carbon copies. Many offices are now using *pc* (for *photocopy*).

Postscript: Studies show that postscripts are one of the first things people read and one of the things they remember, especially when the postscripts are handwritten. They are especially valuable in sales letters. Use postscripts sparingly because they can appear as afterthoughts, indicating a lack of organization. When you do use a postscript notation, place it two lines below your last notation. It isn't necessary to include the abbreviation *P.S.*

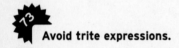

Avoid trite expressions.

When you use stale expressions such as the "Taboos" that follow, you sound like a dinosaur. Replace "Taboos" with "Use."

Taboos	*Use*
As per our conversation	As we discussed
Attached herewith please find	I'm attaching
Awaiting your reply, I remain,	Sincerely,
Enclosed herewith please find	I'm enclosing
I am forwarding herewith	I'm sending
In accordance with your wishes	As you requested
Please don't hesitate to call me	Please call me
Per your request	As you requested
Pursuant to our conversation	As we discussed
Pursuant to your request	As you requested
We are in receipt of	We have received

When you write to an international audience, or to people for whom English is a second language, be mindful of the following:

- Avoid humor, jargon, idioms, and anything that may be misunderstood.
- Write clearly and concisely, but don't oversimplify or talk down to your reader. You don't want to offend.
- Address the reader by her last name, unless you know her well.
- Spell out the date.
- Use international measurement standards (metrics).
- Specify time zones such as Greenwich Mean Time (GMT) or Coordinated Universal Time (UTC), when appropriate.

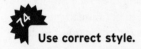

Use correct style.

There are several letter styles. The style may be dictated by your company, or it may be your choice.

Letter Style	Characteristics and Comments
Full Block	Everything starts at the left margin; there's no need to indent.
	Efficient, businesslike, and very popular.
Block (also called Modified Block)	The date, complimentary closing, and signature blocks are slightly to the right of center.
	Everything else starts at the left margin.
	Very traditional and very popular.
Semiblock	Identical to modified block, except the first line of each paragraph is indented.
	This isn't as popular as it once was.

I'm always being asked how to know when to write a letter and when to send an e-mail. Here's an analogy: A letter is to a passionate love affair what an e-mail is to a one-night stand. When you want to woo someone (perhaps to develop a long-term business relationship), send a letter. A letter is warmer and shows more thought. When you want to send something out quickly or casually, send an e-mail.

75

Format a multiple-page letter correctly.

Never crowd your letter onto one page if doing so means narrowing the margins, decreasing the font size, or compromising the visual impact in any way. There's absolutely nothing wrong with an occasional multiple-page letter *when it's necessary*. Here are some tips for presenting a multiple-page letter:

- Use letterhead for the first page and matching plain stationery for subsequent pages.

- When you divide a paragraph between pages, leave at least two lines on the current page and carry over at least two lines to the next page. If the paragraph is very short, put the entire paragraph on the second page.

- Never carry a complimentary closing over to a second page without having at least two lines of text above it.

Following are two examples of how to head a subsequent page of a multiple-page letter:

Second page of a full block letter

| Mark Tetrault | Page 2 | July 2, 20– |

Mark Tetrault
Page 2
July 2, 20–

Strategic Business Letters and E-mail, by Sheryl Lindsell-Roberts (Houghton Mifflin), contains hundreds of model letters you can use verbatim or tweak for your needs. Here are just a few of the categories:

- Sales and Marketing with Pizzazz
- Successful Job Search and Employment Issues
- Customer Relations
- Credit and Collections
- You Are Cordially Invited
- Placing and Acknowledging Orders
- Personal Business Notes
- Media Relations
- Professional Potpourri

E-mails have replaced many of the memos that were once pervasive in the office. However, memos are still used to disseminate information, announce policies, delegate tasks, report results, and more. The body of the memo follows the same format as the body of a letter or e-mail in terms of good business writing. If your office doesn't have predesigned memos, consider using the following format:

LETTERHEAD

Date: November 12, 20–
To: Brian and Jill Ferrick
From: Brooke Riley
Subject: Agenda for November 15 meeting

Italio Catering

300 Main Street • Glenn, GA 30218
phone 012-345-6789 • fax 987-654-3210
www.italiocatering.com

January 21, 20—   ‹Dateline›

CERTIFIED MAIL   ‹Mailing notation›

Mr. Sid Moosnick, CFO
Smorgon Enterprises
304 Heather Lane   ‹Inside address›
Glenn, GA 30219

Dear Mr. Moosnick: ‹Salutation›

Subject: Expanding Our Services to Serve You Better   ‹Subject line›

Thank you for your continued support and confidence in us. Our first priority is to provide you with impeccable service, and we always do our best to make working with us a pleasurable and rewarding experience.

What Else Is New   ‹Body›
In an effort to serve you even better, we've expanded our services and have moved into larger quarters. As you can see by our new letterhead, we're now located at 300 Main Street—only one block from where we were before. Here's what else is new at Italio Catering:

- New equipment
- New ideas to assist you in every aspect of your event planning
- A new policy to have all of our drivers carry cell phones so they can cater to your needs even more efficiently.

As Much as Things Change, They Stay the Same
Italio Catering continues to offer quality you can count on for all your corporate meetings, cocktail receptions, outdoor events, and formal dinners. That's why the *Professional Business Journal* rated us one of the top ten catering companies in the state.

- You see the friendly faces and enjoy the high-quality, flexible service you've come to appreciate.
- You continue to get same-day service.
- When you call during normal business hours, someone answers the phone. Our voice mail operates after hours.

Mr. Sid Moosnick, CFO
Page 2
January 21, 20—

To thank you for your continued confidence in us, please apply the
enclosed $100 gift certificate toward your next function. We look forward
to continuing to partner with you for all your catering needs.

Bon appétit,   <Complimentary closing>

Adele Sharfin

Adele Sharfin   <Signature block>
President

AS/ce   <Reference initials>
Enclosure   <Enclosure notation>
cc: N.M. Mimbres   <Copy notation>

Please send my warmest regards to your
beloved chef, Alfredo!   <Postscript>

*If Columbus had an advisory committee he would
probably still be at the dock.*

ARTHUR GOLDBERG
former US Supreme Court justice

Committees and organizations rely on minutes as an accurate record of what transpires at critical meetings. The minutes provide a permanent record, a reference for reviewing committee decisions, and a recap for those who weren't present. Minutes become an official written record of the meeting and may be used to settle disputes. They must be accurate, complete, and understandable.

 Before you start writing minutes, be certain you've gone through the process in Part One.

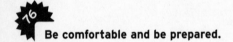

Be comfortable and be prepared.

To record the minutes, use whatever method is comfortable for you. It may be a notepad, laptop, or tape recorder. Be sure to get the names of everyone in the room. If you're unfamiliar with anyone, ask for a business card.

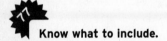

Know what to include.

Although it isn't necessary to record every comment, you must record the key issues and who said what. Think in terms of issues discussed, major points, and decisions. Here are some things to include:

- Essential elements:

      name of the organization
      type of meeting (regular or special)
      date, time, and place
      name of the chair or facilitator
      names of all attendees.

- Statement that the minutes of the previous meeting were approved/revised.

- Unfinished business and reports that were read/approved.

- New business such as major motions. Include whether the motions were carried, defeated, or tabled. Also include the names of those who made and seconded the motions.

- For action items, a list of who needs what and when it's due.

- Full and accurate description of resolutions that were adopted or rejected.

- Date, time, and place of the next meeting.

- Time the meeting adjourned.

If possible, type the minutes while they are fresh in your memory. Then have the chair or facilitator approve the minutes before you distribute them.

78

Standardize your format.

Use a standard format for preparing the minutes. Following is one that uses sidelines so all the categories pop out:

NAME OF ORGANIZATION
Minutes of Monthly Meeting on <Date>
<Place>

Chair:
Present:
Absent:

<Name> called the meeting to order at <time>. <Name> made a motion that the <date of last meeting> minutes be approved and distributed. The motion was seconded by <name> and passed. There is no old business to be discussed.

New Business
   Topic:
   Motion made and seconded:
   Action to be taken:

Good business leaders create a vision,
articulate the vision, passionately own the vision,
and relentlessly drive it to completion.

JACK WELCH
former chairman, General Electric

Successful organizations start with a vision—a mission based on a sense of purpose and realistic goals. When you start a company, one of the first things to do is write a mission statement that crystallizes why you're forming the company. Studies show that companies with mission statements are more profitable than companies without them.

 Before you start your mission statement, be certain you've gone through the process in Part One.

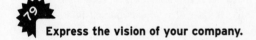

Express the vision of your company.

A mission statement can be a few lines or a few paragraphs that express why your organization exists and what it hopes to achieve. It's a good idea to involve other members of your team to formulate the mission statement (the more input the better). Make sure you believe in your mission. If you don't, your customers or clients will soon realize it.

For-Profit Organization

Following is a mission statement written by a Swedish American marketing team:

> Baystate Connections is poised to deliver marketing services
> to Swedish companies who want a presence in the American
> and Canadian marketplace. These companies will be able to

minimize their overhead because they won't have to hire local staff or relocate personnel. Arrangements can be on a retainer or per-project basis.

Not-for-Profit Organization

Following is a mission statement for a not-for-profit organization to help teens:

> KidsWin is a not-for-profit organization designed to build self-efficacy in teens. The model is to solicit from local business funds to sponsor S.T.A.R. Teens. The expectation is that we are all achievers and have within us the ability to achieve great and wonderful things. As a result of participating in S.T.A.R. Teens, the teens will have better relationships with peers and adults, improved communication skills, and increased capability to meet challenges throughout their lifetimes.

As your company matures, revisit your mission statement to keep yourself on track. It's easy to spread yourself thin and move away from your mission.

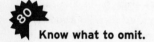

Know what to omit.

In order for your mission statement to provide value, know what to omit.

- Avoid saying how great you are or that you intend to be a leading provider. Those words are meaningless. (Everyone thinks they're great and wants to be a leading provider.)

- Avoid buzzwords and jargon.

- Your mission statement is intended to keep you on track. It's meant to be an internal document. Don't plaster it on your brochures or website.

*If you think publicity doesn't pay, there are 25 mountains
in Colorado higher than Pikes Peak. Can you name one?*

ANONYMOUS

A press release is one of the most powerful forms of advertising and marketing on the planet. Nothing builds credibility more than a well-written press release that gets picked up by a newspaper, magazine, or the Internet. The publicity will increase sales, expose your company to the masses, and enhance your image.

There are many opportunities for issuing press releases. Local publications often print press releases when a company opens a business, moves to a new location, hires a new employee, expands its facilities, holds a fundraising drive, bestows an honor, and more. Large publications publish press releases that are of specific interest to their demographic groups.

 Before you start writing your press release, be certain you've gone through the process in Part One.

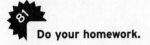

Do your homework.

You don't need to hire a public relations agency to write a press release. You can write your own and send it to newspapers, magazines, and/or broadcasting stations. Build an accurate database of contacts, and keep the list current because editors tend to move around.

- **Become familiar with the publications you target.** Read them. Get a sense of their styles and tones.

- **Write to a specific editor.** The editors' names are listed on the masthead of a publication. If you can't find a name, call the publication and ask for a specific editor.

- **Send copy that's error-free.** You build trust with the media when you send an accurate story that has no typos or misinformation.

- **Remember that editors often respond quickly.** If your press release is timely, an editor may respond quickly. Be sure you respond quickly also.

- **Be aware of deadlines.** Some publications require as much as three months' lead time. Check with the publication, especially if your story is time-sensitive.

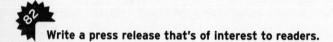

Write a press release that's of interest to readers.

When you write the press release, consider how it's of interest to your target audience. You won't get your press release published in a paper publication if you're peddling your company's success story. (That's why publications sell advertising space.) Instead ask yourself, What value is this to readers?

- **Leave your ego at the door.** The publication doesn't aim to help you make money or drive visitors to your website. Rather, it's looking for a story that will interest its readers.

- **Avoid red flags.** When sending by e-mail (and most press releases are submitted by e-mail), omit words such as *mortgage rates*, *free*, *sexy*, and others along those lines, in the subject line. They may appear to be spam and get blocked by filters.

- **Write from a journalist's perspective.** Avoid *I* or *we* unless it's in a quote.

- **Avoid industry lingo.** Although lingo may be widespread in your industry, you must first attract the attention of an editor. Lingo may be a sure-fire turnoff. Therefore, you must strike a balance between a relatively uninformed editor and an informed reader.

- **Include a photo, when appropriate.** People's eyes are drawn to graphics and text, more than to text alone.

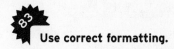 Write with a flair that will interest readers, rather than with the same boring text you see all the time. Notice the difference in the examples below:

Flair: One hundred future business leaders were feted at a black-tie ceremony in New York City. The event was attended by several CIOs who gathered from across the globe.

Boring: Two hundred CEOs attended a dinner in New York City to honor 100 future business leaders.

83

Use correct formatting.

Write your press release in *decreasing* order of importance. Answer *who, what, when, where, why,* and *how* in the first paragraph, just as reporters do. Follow these guidelines and check out the example on page 120.

- **FOR IMMEDIATE RELEASE:** Put these words, in all caps or large and small caps, in the upper left margin or in the center.

- **Contact information:** Include the name, title, phone, and company spokesperson. *Be sure the information is accurate.* A large travel agency recently published a special deal and transposed two digits in its phone number. People who called reached a sex hotline. (This was an ad, not a press release, but you get the picture.)

- **Headline:** Write the headline in bold. Use this as an opportunity to summarize the information in the press release in a way that's exciting and dynamic.

- **Lead paragraph:** Pay close attention to Tip 11, on using the questioning technique. When you write as a reporter writes and include the key information in the first paragraph, you increase your odds of getting published.

- **Text:** Follow the lead paragraph with the fully developed message.

- **Number of words:** Include the number of words in parentheses at the bottom.

- **Start and end with # # # #.** These symbols indicate the beginning and end.

Press release (paper)

FOR IMMEDIATE RELEASE

# # # #

LOCAL ARCHITECT OPENS NEW OFFICE

Marc A. Lindsell, President of Marc Lindsell Architecture, is pleased to announce the opening of his new office at 501 Cortland Street in San Francisco. Marc settled in the Bay Area 12 years ago after graduating from Georgia Institute of Technology College of Architecture.

Marc started his career designing schools and municipal buildings and opened his own firm 9 years ago, specializing in new home design and remodeling. Marc's uniquely designed homes have been featured in the Home section of the *Sunday Boston Globe* and in *Architectural Record*, a prestigious publication for architects. Marc is also the winner of several awards presented by the National Association of the Remodeling Industry (NARI) for remodeling projects. You can contact Marc at 415-826-5459.

(125 words)

# # # #

If you don't get your press release published, send it to the same editor a second time. After the second attempt, follow up with a phone call. If that doesn't work, don't lose hope. Persistence often pays off. You never know what will capture someone's attention.

Use the power of the Internet.

Posting a press release on the Internet is a wonderful way to reach massive numbers of people worldwide. Unlike a paper press release, you can use a sales pitch and a less structured format.

As mentioned in Tip 25, I recently posted the following press release on the Internet to advertise my online e-mail workshop. As in a website, you need to include keywords so people can find you. Notice that I use both *email* and *e-mail* to capture audiences who use one or the other. This press release got 19,000 clicks the first week.

Press release (Internet)

Back   Forward   Stop   Refresh   Home   Print   Mail

Online Workshops to Turn Your Email into a Productive Business Tool
Protect yourself by understanding the legalities of email and grow your business through effective email messaging—anytime—anywhere—at your own pace—at affordable prices.

In two interactive online workshops, you receive top-flight instruction filled with practical examples and realistic situations such as how to deliver your message in the subject line and how to avoid crossing the legal line. This is a fast and cost-effective way to get training and get results.

E-mails that Mean Business—$49.95 per user

Learn how to write an effective message that gets read and gets results. Participants will learn to
- write a compelling e-mail subject line
- use the basics of e-mail etiquette
- compose an e-mail that is not only read, but gets the desired action.

E-mails that Avoid Legal Pitfalls—$49.95 per user

E-mails are permanent records and can come back to hurt you. Learn to identify the do's and don'ts of e-mails and avoid unintended legal consequences. Participants will learn to recognize and respond to e-mails
- that create or modify legal agreements
- that "cross the line" and could be evidence of harassment.

Both workshops—$74.95 per user—Volume discounts are available.

ACT NOW!

For more information and/or a demo, email info@techcomm-partners.com or call 401-568-5816. These workshops are a great investment. You'll greatly increase the effectiveness of email and learn how to avoid common mistakes. (It cost Goldman Sachs $2 million for improperly offering securities through email.)

About the Workshop Facilitators

Sheryl Lindsell-Roberts is an award-winning business writer, author of 19 books, and workshop facilitator who works with large and small companies to transform the way they communicate. She has helped clients to close multimillion-dollar contracts. Sheryl's workshops are nationally acclaimed by companies and universities such as EMC, Tufts University, Babcock Power Environmental, IDG, Baycare Health Partners, and others. Sheryl's website is www.sherylwrites.com.

Workshop leader **Jean Sifleet** is a business attorney and CPA whose career spans many years in large multinational corporations and includes three successful entrepreneurial ventures. She teaches business law and has authored two books and many publications on avoiding legal pitfalls in business. Her website www.smartfast.com is a recognized resource for practical information on business issues.

*The most important parts of any talk are
the beginning and the end. And they should be
as close together as possible.*

GEORGE BURNS

As part of the business community, you'll undoubtedly be called upon to prepare and/or deliver a presentation. Broad categories include management briefings, peer group meetings, trade shows, conventions, customer presentations, and more. Think of your presentation as an opportunity to get out from behind your desk and shine.

Remember that every time you make a presentation, your audience receives and evaluates hundreds of subtle audio and visual cues you reveal to them. This helps them to form opinions regarding you, your product or service, and your company. Use this power to your advantage. Provide a forum to *sell* yourself, your ideas, your department, or your company. A good presentation will be very valuable to your career.

 Before you start writing your PowerPoint presentation, be certain you've gone through the process in Part One.

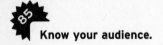

Know your audience.

To build rapport with your audience, ask yourself the following:

- Who are they?
- What do they *need to know* about the topic?
- What are their expectations?
- What are my expectations?

If your audience is diverse, pinpoint common threads such as shared interests, related professions, socioeconomic characteristics. After all, everyone is there for a common reason.

86
Use the power of persuasion.

Your persuasiveness comes through in the way you organize the material. Your ability to analyze, organize, and motivate should be evident in the way you present your material—visually and orally. Here are pointers for making your presentation persuasive:

- Start with a summary—a brief overview to give your audience a clear idea of what your presentation covers.
- State the problem or need.
- Solve the audience's problem or need by making recommendations.
- Back up your recommendations. Be prepared to deal with questions or objections.
- Gently push for action.
- Summarize your main points, starting each point with an action word (a verb).

How many slides should you include? There's no easy answer to that; however, presenters generally prepare and show too many. You may want to use this rule of thumb: However many you prepare, cut that in half and see if you can still convey your message.

87
Distinguish between what to include in the visuals and what to say.

Always keep in mind that your audience attends your presentation to listen to you. *Your visuals are your aids, not your focus.* They should support what you say, not mimic what you say. No one wants to listen to a talking head. One way to put the focus on yourself is to introduce your visuals. For example, you might say, "The following slide is a diagram that shows . . ." In that way *you* maintain the focus and the visual becomes your aid.

Use visuals to clarify ideas, emphasize key points, show relationships, and provide supporting information. Present the big picture. Audiences remember concepts, trends, and impressions, not raw data and minutiae.

- Prepare a master slide so the slides all have the same fonts, colors, and banner.
- Include your logo on all slides.
- If you make a presentation to a client or potential client, include the client's logo. This is very important for creating goodwill.
- Rather than using just text, add interesting images when appropriate.

Prepare one visual for each point.

Each visual should address one of these questions:

- What is it?
- What are the benefits?
- Where is it?
- How much is there?
- How does it work?
- What are the parameters?

If the slide doesn't answer one of these questions or another critical question, ask yourself if you really need it. (Check out Tip 91 to see how a storyboard can help to tell your story.)

89

Craft text strategically.

Your text must be read easily from the worst seat in the room.

- Craft headlines that make the visual readable and grab the audience's attention.
- Use active, high-impact words. If possible, prominently display the words *you* or *your*.
- Use upper- and lowercase, even for the headlines.
- Limit visuals to five to seven lines of text. (Check out the *After* and *Before* slides on pages 130–131.)
- Include bulleted or numbered lists. (Check out Tip 18 to understand the difference between bullets and numbers.)
- Use a 24-point font for the headlines and an 18-point font for the text.

90

Use graphics to enhance the message.

Remembering that a picture is worth a thousand words, try these suggestions:

- Show pictures, diagrams, and charts to aid comprehension. This is especially helpful when presenting technical or complex issues.
- Use lines, shapes, and colors to clarify your message.
- When preparing charts, label axes and data lines.
- Create a legend to explain a graphic.
- Use a picture to jazz up an otherwise dull slide. See the following example.

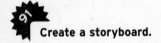

Start-Up Strategies

❖ Outlining
❖ Using index cards
❖ Questioning
❖ Brainstorming
❖ Freewriting

 Don't let the visuals overpower the text or draw attention away from you. Keep them simple, as in the preceding slide.

91

Create a storyboard.

A storyboard is a visual display that tells your story. It lets you see the continuity of your slides to determine whether you told too much or your story has gaps. Here's how to set up a storyboard:

1. Create two columns.
2. Populate the left column with your topics—the slide headings.
3. Populate the right column with the supporting text.

Storyboard

Step 1: Getting Started	• Use the Start Up Sheet. • Use the questioning technique.
Step 2: Creating Headlines and Sequencing Strategically	• Write compelling and informational headlines. • Sequence headlines for maximum impact.
Step 3: Writing the Draft	• Get ready to write the draft. • Write the draft. • Revisit the draft.
Step 4: Designing for Visual Impact	• Use white space properly. • Use bullets, numbers, tables, and charts. • Understand the use of color.
Step 5: Honing the Tone	• Put your personality on paper. • Keep it short and simple. • Use the active voice. • Use positive words and phrases.
Step 6: Proofreading	• Proofread until your eyeballs hurt. • Use your electronic tools.

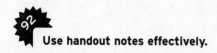

Use handout notes effectively.

Use notes to enhance your message so you don't crowd slides. The *After* slide on page 130 contains the right amount of text; notes provide further explanations and may be printed on the same sheet of paper. The *Before* slide on page 131 has too much text.

Stencil-Printed Wafer Bumps

- Electroforming process needs updating
- Upgrading metrology requires capital investment
- Cleanroom and other facilities need updating
- Quality system needs upgrading

Notes:

Electroforming process needs updating

- Stencil cleaning
- Lithography
- Pattern effects limit uniformity

Upgrading metrology requires capital investment

- 100% inspection on finished stencil
- Pre-plate resist inspection
- Stencil thickness metrology

Cleanroom and other facilities need updating

- Stencil handling
- Airborne particles
- Air conditioning

Quality system needs upgrading

- PM program
- SPC

Stencil-Printed Wafer Bumps

Electroforming process needs updating
- Stencil cleaning
- Lithography
- Pattern effects limit uniformity

Upgrading metrology requires capital investment
- 100% inspection on finished stencil
- Pre-plate resist inspection
- Stencil thickness metrology

Cleanroom and other facilities need updating
- Stencil handling
- Airborne particles
- Air conditioning

Quality system needs upgrading
- PM program
- SPC

 Keep in mind these presentation do's and taboos.

Do's	Taboos
■ Show up early.	■ Don't leave your laptop turned on in standby mode.
■ Check the equipment. (Never assume your presentation will work on someone else's laptop.)	■ Don't leave your screensaver on.
■ Face your audience as much as possible.	■ Don't engage in frequent mouse or keyboard interaction.

Use the following checklist for presentations:

- ☐ Is my purpose crystal clear?
- ☐ Did I learn everything I can about my audience?
- ☐ Did I distinguish between what to say and what to project?
- ☐ Are my visuals informative and pleasing to look at?
- ☐ Can my visuals be seen from the worst seat in the room?
- ☐ Have I organized my presentation into logical topics and subtopics?
- ☐ Have I practiced my presentation in front of a mirror or before peers?
- ☐ Have I anticipated questions?
- ☐ Am I prepared to answer them?
- ☐ Have I confirmed the date, time, and place of the presentation?

Check out the facilities as soon as you arrive. A colleague of mine did a training session at a hotel, and the conference room had no phone jacks. He needed to hook up computers and ended up stringing a phone line across the lobby, hanging it from the grids in the suspended ceiling. He can never show his face in that hotel again.

*So we went to Atari and said, "Hey, we've got this
amazing thing, even built with some of your parts, and
what do you think about funding us? Or we'll give it to
you. We just want to do it. Pay our salary, we'll come to
work for you." And they said no. So then we went to
Hewlett-Packard, and they said, "Hey, we don't need you.
You haven't gotten through college yet."*

STEVE JOBS
cofounder of Apple Computer, Inc.

You write a proposal to provide goods or services to a potential buyer
within a certain amount of time at a specified cost. This is unlike a grant
where you ask for funding. Your proposal may be in the format of an
internal memo where you propose a change or improvement within your
company. Or your proposal may be external where you're asked to solve
someone else's problem. In either case, your goal is to write a proposal
that's convincing.

Before you start writing your proposal, be certain you've gone
through the process in Part One.

Write a convincing internal proposal.

An internal proposal generally recommends change or improvement
within a company. This can range from a simple plan to expand cafeteria
services to a detailed plan for an overhaul of the management reporting
system. The proposal is sent to a higher-ranking person who has the
authority to accept or reject it.

- Open an internal proposal with the problem that needs a solution.

- Include the following in the body:

    Practical solution
    Breakdown of the costs
    Information about equipment, materials, personnel
    Schedule for completing the tasks.

- Conclude with a brief recap of the recommendations. In a spirit of cooperation, consider asking for a meeting.

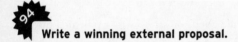

Write a winning external proposal.

An external proposal responds to a need outside your company. The proposal may follow a request for proposal (RFP), a request for quote (RFQ), or a less formal set of guidelines. For an external proposal, consider this format:

Front Matter

Include the following:

- **Transmittal letter.** Express your appreciation for the chance to submit your proposal. Acknowledge any previous experience with the customer (assuming it was positive), and summarize the recommendations you will make.

- **Title page.** Use high-quality paper that's thicker than the inside pages. When you can, include the prospect's logo. If the proposal is for a large project, it's worthwhile having a graphic artist design a great-looking cover. Remember that first impressions count! Following are two example title pages:

Proposal Prepared Expressly for

PROSPECT'S LOGO

Submitter's Name
Title
City, State

Name of Project
Date of Submission

YOUR LOGO

YOUR LOGO

Welcomes the Opportunity to
Partner with

PROSPECT'S LOGO

Submitter's Name
Title
City, State

Name of Project
Date of Submission

 Make the
prospect's
logo larger than
yours.

Introduction

Limit the introduction to 200 words. Include upbeat information that sells you or your company. Review marketing materials and include what makes your company the one to be selected. Include a graphic, if appropriate.

Executive Summary

Give the highlights of the proposal that "sell" you or your company. (Check out Executive Summaries, beginning on page 83, for more details.)

Table of Contents

Prepare an annotated table of contents that breaks everything out clearly.

Body

Include from the following what's relevant to your proposal:

- Methodology
- Equipment recommended
- Detailed cost analysis
- Delivery schedule
- Summary of advantages/benefits
- Statement of responsibilities
- Description of vendor
- Advertising literature
- Conclusions or recommendations.

Back Matter

Include from the following what's relevant to your proposal:

- Bibliography
- Qualifications/Resumes
- Appendices
- Glossary of terms.

Check out the Grants section, beginning on page 89, for further details on external proposals.

Include why the prospect should select you over other candidates.

Make it crystal clear to the prospect that you stand tall above the competition.

- If the proposal is for a product, stress what benefits your product offers that the competitor's product doesn't. (Check out Tip 126 for a discussion of the differences between benefits and features.)

- If the proposal is for a service, stress the applicable credentials and talents of your team.

- Highlight previous, similar projects that you brought in under budget or ahead of schedule.

Don't use the same boring phrases everyone else uses, such as "We have an experienced team of people and highly qualified management." What company would say "We have an inexperienced team of people and unqualified management"?

Get to know the RFP or RFQ.

Many proposals are driven by an RFP or RFQ. Government agencies often solicit bids with an invitation for bids (IFB). Following are suggestions for writing a proposal in response to any of these:

- **Read the RFP or RFQ thoroughly several times.** You must understand all the ramifications.

- **Read between the lines.** It may be necessary to read between the lines to discover hints to approaching the project. Those who write RFPs and RFQs aren't necessarily good writers, and they may not express things carefully or fully. If there are parts you don't understand, contact the prospect. It's best to get the responses in writing (if possible), because verbal information isn't binding.

- **Prepare a checklist.** This will help you to focus on exactly what's required for each item.

- **Be open about providing alternatives.** When you identify the pitfalls of a solution or a more cost-effective way to solve a problem, you set yourself apart from other bidders. First, however, respond to what the document asks for, then propose an alternative.

- **Put the RFP or RFQ in a three-ring binder.** Use insert dividers or self-stick notes to mark important pages or paragraphs.

It's important to let the prospect know you included everything asked for. *Use the prospect's words.* Following are two suggested formats for recapping:

Recapping prospect's requirements in the transmittal letter

Professional Qualifications

The following are our qualifications as outlined in your RFP. We've included the corresponding page numbers, so you can find the information quickly:

1. <State> registration and licensing in all applicable disciplines (page__).

2. Thorough knowledge of procedures, requirements, and practices of the <state> State Board of Education, School Governance Bureau, and other agencies related to the design and construction of schools (page__).

3. Thorough knowledge of the <state> State Building Code and Regulations Architectural Barriers Board (page__).

For a lengthy proposal, attach a table such as the following to the transmittal letter and mention that it supplements the table of contents.

Recapping prospect's requirements on a separate sheet

Item	Description	Page
01	Bidder's principal contact	1
02	Proposal price breakdown	1
03	Resumes of team members	3

Sometimes requestors seek proposals in areas they know nothing about. If you have a fire in your belly for the job, educating the requestor is a winning strategy.

I was writing a proposal in response to an RFP to prepare a video. The RFP was sketchy at best. I called the requesting agency and asked for more details; they weren't giving out any additional information. However, I did find out that the people who would be evaluating the proposals didn't know squat about preparing a video.

From my past experience, I know that people don't appreciate how much time and work goes into producing a video. I wanted to educate the people who would be evaluating my proposal to justify the cost. Therefore, I started the proposal with "The Basics of a Video Production," a section that explained what happens during each stage of video production.

I was the only submitter who took the time to explain the video production process. Although my bid was slightly higher than some of the others, I was awarded the contract.

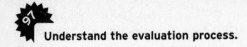

Understand the evaluation process.

Find out how the prospect plans to evaluate proposals. Prospects are often willing to share this information, but you must ask for it. The more you know in advance, the better prepared you are. Remember that the contract doesn't necessarily go to the lowest bidder; it often goes to the one who can solve the prospect's business problem. Here are some questions to ask the prospect:

- Is there a formal scoring mechanism?
- What qualities are scored?
- How much weight is given to each quality?
- How many people are reviewing the proposal?
- What level of knowledge do the evaluators have about what we're proposing?

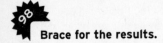

Brace for the results.

If you win, break out a bottle of champagne. If you lose, don't get discouraged. No one wins all the time. Call to request an in-person or telephone briefing to find out why you lost. (A briefing may or may not be granted.) Learn from the experience and apply that learning to your next proposal. Proposals often fail because they didn't

- Present a professional look
- Follow instructions in the RFP or RFQ
- Include all the information requested
- Demonstrate an understanding of the problem
- Take evaluation criteria into consideration
- Specify their approach clearly enough
- Meet the prospect's budgetary constraints
- Include relevant information about their firm and its people
- Stress the benefits they offer that their competitors don't
- Meet the deadline.

Jane, president of an architectural firm, had a chance to bid on a multimillion-dollar project, and she was determined to win the contract. In response to the RFP, Jane decided to go out on a limb and differentiate her company. Instead of preparing a traditional proposal, she prepared a professional video showing why the prospect should select her firm.

Jane selected the projects of which she was most proud. She videotaped the architectural drawings, finished buildings, and testimonials. She morphed between before and after renovations. She also scrolled resumes (to music) of those who would be involved in the project. Jane then purchased a new DVD player and inserted the DVD into the slot. She wrapped the package and hired a messenger to deliver it to the prospective client.

As you probably guessed, Jane's company got the contract. After the contract was signed, the prospect admitted that his company was so impressed with Jane's creativity that he didn't even consider anyone else.

Sometimes creativity can make you fall flat on your face. Other times, it can get you the brass ring. Just ask Jane!

QUESTIONNAIRES

The census is taken by the Census Bureau every ten years,
as required by the Constitution. (For the other nine years,
Census Bureau employees play pinochle while remaining
on Red Alert, in case the Constitution suddenly changes.)

DAVE BARRY
"Counting the House," *The Boston Globe*

A questionnaire (also called an evaluation form or survey) is an interview on paper. Your goal is to get as much information as you can while requiring minimal effort on the part of those being questioned. Keep the questionnaire as brief as possible. The longer it is, the less likely that people will complete it. Questionnaires are commonly used to

- Evaluate the success of a workshop, seminar, or presentation
- Measure job satisfaction (this type of questionnaire is sometimes called a pulse survey)
- Understand readers' needs
- Anticipate the success of a new product or service
- Determine whether a client's expectations were met.

 Before you start writing your questionnaire, be certain you've gone through the process in Part One.

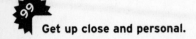

Get up close and personal.

Face-to-face and telephone questionnaires give the interviewer an opportunity to follow up on answers and delve more deeply into details. They are a great way to speak with people personally to ask what they think of an idea or product. This type of questioning, however, is limited to the number of people the interviewer can reach, so the results don't always represent a large cross section of people.

Some people are put off by face-to-face questionnaires because those being questioned sit there twiddling their thumbs while the interviewer jots down every word. (For example, we've all been stopped by people in shopping malls who want to "take just a few minutes" of our time. Three hours later we're still held captive.) Also, many people are put off by telephone questionnaires. We all get far too many telemarketing calls, and a telephone interview is just one more.

100 Realize the benefits of mail or Web questionnaires.

There are advantages to questionnaires that are mailed or posted on the Web. A key advantage is that the interviewer can't influence an answer by facial expressions or tone of voice. Therefore, the results tend to be more unbiased. One key disadvantage is that people with strong opinions are more likely to respond, so results get skewed. Another drawback is that there's no opportunity for someone to follow up with a pertinent question that may shed more light on a subject.

Be aware that the anonymity of the Web may lead to some bizarre responses because it's so easy to type something and click to send. People occasionally use anonymity as an opportunity to sound off on issues that may not relate directly to the topic at hand.

> ■ I was at a client's office recently and a computer programmer told me he wrote a short questionnaire to get feedback for online help. Someone took the opportunity to rant and rave that the company's stock had gone down dramatically. Someone else didn't like the food in the cafeteria.
>
> ■ A website was posted for students to evaluate their professors. One student anonymously wrote in that the book was a better teacher than the professor and it had a better personality.

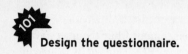

Design the questionnaire.

Keep the form simple and brief. You want respondents to give you lots of information with minimum time and effort. Here are some nifty tips on preparing the questions:

- **Let respondents know the questionnaire is for their benefit, not yours.** Consider a beginning like this:

    > Prestige Company is constantly striving to provide you with the highest quality. We value your opinion and hope you'll take a few minutes to let us know what you think of this manual.

- **Word the questions so they're straightforward, not vague.**

    Straightforward: Have you found any content errors? If you have, please identify the error and page number.
    Vague: Have you found any errors?

- **Arrange the questions so those easiest to answer come at the beginning.** Some respondents don't bother to read much beyond the first few questions, so get them while you have their attention.

- **Group items about the same subject together.** This makes it easier for respondents to answer the questions and easier for you to tally the responses.

- **Provide space for additional comments.** If you're not sure you addressed all possible issues, give the respondents a chance to write their own comments. You'd be surprised at how much you find out. Consider a section like this:

    > Please let us know how we may make this manual more valuable. We welcome additional comments. Please write on the back if you need more space.

- **Deal with confidentiality.** If the questionnaire may prove embarrassing or the results need to be private for some reason, clearly assure the respondents that their answers will be confidential, and be sure they are!

- **Let the respondents know how to return the questionnaire.** If you're not on hand to collect the form, provide a fax number, e-mail address, or a self-addressed, stamped envelope.

Questionnaires typically contain two types of questions: closed-ended and open-ended. Some people respond well to one type and not the other, so consider creating a balance.

Closed-ended questions

Closed-ended questions ask respondents to select from predefined answers that are closest to their viewpoints. They may be yes or no, true or false, multiple choice, or a sliding scale.

- **Yes or no questions** require minimal effort on the part of the respondent:

> Would you recommend this book to your friends?
>
> ☐ Yes ☐ No ☐ Not sure

- When you'd like more elaboration, consider **multiple-choice questions.** The following example gives respondents a number of choices:

> How quickly do you expect the Help Desk to return phone calls?
>
> ☐ Immediately
> ☐ Within one hour
> ☐ Within two hours
> ☐ Within one day
> ☐ Other _____

- A **sliding scale** gives respondents a chance to reply within a range:

Workshop Content				
I received the tools to	Excellent	Good	Fair	Poor
1. Write documents that get attention.				
2. Help my reader find the key issues quickly.				
3. Express my ideas more clearly and concisely.				
4. Get started more easily.				

If you use a numbered scale, let respondents know which end of the scale is high and which is low. You might include the following:

    1 = Always   3 = Infrequently
    2 = Frequently   4 = Never

Closed-ended questions are easier to answer and tabulate than open-ended questions, but they don't allow respondents to elaborate.

Open-ended questions

Open-ended questions, such as the one below, let respondents answer in their own words. They are useful because you can get a lot of valuable feedback from explanations.

Would you recommend this seminar to others? Please tell us why or why not. _____

_____

_____

Some respondents, however, don't take the time to answer open-ended questions. That's why a mix of closed- and open-ended questions strikes a balance.

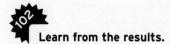

Learn from the results.

When the results of the questionnaire are glowing or you get the answers you expect, don't rest on your laurels. There are always ways you can improve. When the embers aren't glowing, rise from the ashes and learn from the responses. Always regard disapproving comments as a way to reach a higher level of excellence.

Remember, *information is power!* A well-designed client/customer questionnaire can give you the following feedback:

- Firsthand knowledge of how respondents perceive you and your company
- How you can improve the quality of your product or service
- Untapped areas for providing additional service
- The strengths and weaknesses of a new idea, new pricing strategies, and more
- Referrals from respondents' colleagues.

RESUMES

Work is the curse of the drinking class.

OSCAR WILDE

The resume itself won't get you a job; it's a door opener to get you an interview. With a little effort and the following tips, you can write a resume that makes you stand out as a superior candidate for the job you're seeking. See pages 153–154 for a sample resume.

 Before you start writing your resume, be certain you've gone through the process in Part One.

Start with a summary of your qualifications.

Starting resumes with "Objectives" or "Professional Objectives" was the norm years ago. However, meaningless, plain, vanilla statements such as "To use my education and marketing experience in a dynamic work environment" are a big yawn. Instead, start with "Professional Highlights" or "Career Summary" to capture a few relevant career highlights at the top of the page. Quantify these highlights with numbers and percentages when you can. Here's an example:

Professional Highlights

For the past 20 years I have worked in the high-tech field for Fortune 500 companies and have spearheaded many successful marketing campaigns. Here are some specifics:

- Directed a marketing campaign for <product> that brought in $1.5 million in new business.
- Supervised a full-time staff of 12 and a part-time staff of 18.
- Managed three separate budgets of more than $550,000.

Although the cut-your-hair mentality no longer rules the business world, not everything goes. If you submit your resume online and send it from your in_hot_pursuit_daddyo23@aol.com (or something similar) account, your resume will go straight into the recycle bin. Consider setting up two separate accounts—one for fun and one for business. Here are some other ways to tip the scales in your favor:

* Avoid graphics, boxes, bullets, underlining, and italics. (Replace boxes with a stream of hyphens, bullets with asterisks, and underlining and italics with boldface.)

* Use simple fonts such as Times Roman or Ariel.

* Save the document using the .txt extension.

* Include a list of keywords to open your resume so the scanner sees you as a suitable candidate. A keyword list should look like this:

   Keywords: Semiconductor, process engineer, thin films, PVD, PECVD, etching, silicon, applications, vacuum, solder bumping, flip chip.

* E-mail your resume to a friend or colleague. Ask that person to forward it back to you so you can see how it looks. This will show if you need to rework anything.

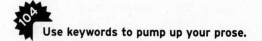

104 Use keywords to pump up your prose.

When you write your resume, pepper it with action words that bring to mind a range of transferable skills:

achieved	managed
administered	negotiated

budgeted	organized
created	saved
empowered	sold
headed	structured
increased	supervised
installed	systematized
instructed	updated

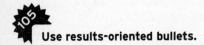

Use results-oriented bullets.

Busy employers find long paragraphs difficult to read and will often gloss over them. Replace run-on text with bullets. Focus bulleted items on specific results, rather than on general tasks.

Results-oriented: Directed a staff of 15 in the daily operation of a $3.5 million business.

Task-oriented: Handled all aspects of the operation.

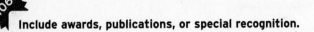

Include awards, publications, or special recognition.

Include awards or special recognition for anything outstanding.

- Were you ever employee of the month?
- Were you honored for an industry accomplishment?
- Have you had anything published in a professional journal?
- Have you presented at a professional conference?

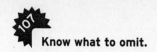

Know what to omit.

Here are a few hints as to what to leave off your resume:

- **Trite phrases such as "I have a good personality" or "I'm reliable."** Would anyone actually say "I have a lousy personality" or "I'm unreliable"?

- **References.** Prospective employers won't check your references until they've met you and judged you a strong candidate. And there's no need to say that references will be furnished upon request. That's understood.

- **Hobbies.** Include hobbies only if they're relevant to the position.

- **Personal information.** There's no need to mention height, weight, age, date of birth, place of birth, marital status, sex, ethnicity, race, health, social security number, religious or political affiliations, or to provide a photo.

- **Lies.** Background checks will fail you.

- **Salary information.** Save that for the interview.

- **Reason for leaving a job.** Save that for the interview.

Never underestimate the appearance of your resume. Use a good-quality printer and high-quality paper. Allow for ample white space. Highlight key points with bullets.

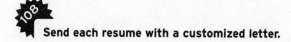

Send each resume with a customized letter.

Take the time to personalize each letter by researching the company and considering the skills needed to perform the position you're after. This will set you apart from other candidates and increase your chances for an interview. Here are a few hints for personalizing your letter:

- Limit the letter to three paragraphs.

Opening paragraph Open with how you learned of the position, or mention the person who referred you.

Middle paragraph Elaborate on a few key "selling points" mentioned in your resume.

Closing paragraph This is a call to action. Request an interview. Say that you'll follow up by phone.

- Match your strengths to the skills the job requires. If you answer an ad, mention that you have the skills the employer asks for.

- Show that you understand the position and the company.

- Use some boilerplate phrases (such as in the closing paragraph), but individualize each letter to meet the needs of the position you're after.

- Close with the request for an interview.

Jane Doe

janedoe@aol.com

508-666-3334
5 Westminster Road, Marlborough, MA 01752

Professional Highlights

Accomplished software engineer with extensive experience in Linux, Windows NT, Device Drivers, and Enterprise-class storage systems. Five years' experience in product marketing with a comprehensive understanding of the business issues of software development from vision to market launch. Proven track record working in both small and large development environments.

- Created and developed a new product to manage DataComm's Roncal storage subsystem that was later adopted by Roncal.
- Managed a small group of young developers at SpeakEasy that resulted in the development of three new speech recognition applications and a new version of the speech recognition engine.
- At Quartell, with a very small development group, created and developed a new thin-server appliance. Accomplished this in less than six months.

Technical Expertise

- *Languages:* C/C++, AWK, bash, make, CVS, RCS, postscript, groff, lex, yacc
- *Operating Systems:* Redhat Linux 6.0–7.3, WINDOWS/NT, WIN32 API, Unix (V.4.2)
- *Interfaces:* i2c, SCSI, ATA, SCSI tape and media changer, SNMP, ONC/RPC

Professional Experience

Quartell | ATZ, Worcester, MA, 1997–present

Staff Engineer – Reporting to Quartell / ATZ CTO
Designed, procured, and managed a new development lab. Responsible for the lab, office systems and local area network for 30 systems and 8 engineers.

Lead Engineer for DX30, an embedded Linux virtual tape library, launched fall of 2002
- Codeveloped a working proof-of-concept of the virtual library with multiple tape drives and changer. Demonstrated to Quartell CEO and executive staff resulting in corporate commitment and funding for the project.
- Developed Linux device drivers including Q Fibre Channel running in SCSI target mode, Hant 24x4 LCD display, system monitoring of temperature, fans, and voltages using LM87 and LM75, and a high performance buffer manager between the Fibre channel and Linux I/O subsystem. Enhanced standard Linux USB 2.0 and RAID5 drivers.

Jane Doe
Page 2

SpeakEasy, Inc., Nashua, NH 1996-1997

Three-year-old start-up specializing in speech recognition software, purchased by VCS in 1997, later purchased by Philips N.V.

Director of Engineering
- Directed all engineering efforts for rev 2.0 release of Automatic Speech
  Recognition Software and succeeded in shipping product on time.
- Developed customer documentation, training; managed beta program.
- Established product teams, managed product plans and schedules.
  Working closely with marketing, obtained customer feedback.

Principal Engineer for port to NT 4.0
- Led the engineering effort to port ASR software from SCO Unix to
  Windows/NT, forcing a major redesign of the internal architecture to support Win32 threads and DLL modules.
- Defined and developed network-based regression and stress-test system
  for ASR software. System simulated more than 20 simultaneous phone
  calls and measured major aspects of system performance with a repeata-
  bility within 2%.

DataComm Corporation, Greenfield, MA 1980-1996

Fortune 500 mini-computer manufacturer with worldwide operations

*Software Staff Specialist, Network Systems Engineering Division,
1992-1996*
- Conceptualized, obtained corporate commitment for, designed, implemented, and shipped an ONC/RPC and SNMP-based agent to manage a
  proprietary disk array (Roncal) on Unix and Windows/NT systems.
  Evolved into EMC's Navisphere product.
- Developed extensions to ONC/RPC to provide asynchronous operation
  for a Unix clustering product.
- Provided significant amount of custom engineering for major federal
  opportunity for network management.

Education

BS/CS from Purdue University, West Lafayette, Indiana. 3.5 Major GPA.

*This report, by its very length, defends itself
against the risk of being read.*

SIR WINSTON CHURCHILL

A report is an impartial and objective presentation of facts used to assist in decision making. A report can range from a simple one-pager a schoolchild writes as a homework assignment to a several-hundred-page feasibility study, investigative report, progress report, trip report, seminar report, trouble report, or more. A report must be skillfully planned and organized, logically sequenced, objective, accurate, reliable, and easy to read. Reports can travel by several routes:

- **Downward from managers to support staff.** Managers use reports to inform the "troops" of decisions being implemented.

- **From peer to peer.** Peers prepare reports to coordinate activities or keep the lines of communication flowing.

- **From a person or committee up the management ranks.** Managers can't participate in all department activities. Reports provide them with information to make informed decisions.

- **From inside the organization to outside the organization.** Reports to customers or stockholders fall into this category.

 Before you start writing your report, be certain you've gone through the process in Part One.

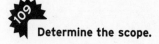

109 Determine the scope.

One mistake report writers typically make is being too general or too vague. Limit the information to the most needed and most important.

For example, if you are reporting on ways to improve employee morale, narrow the scope to salaries, fringe benefits, assignments, hours, evaluation procedures, and recognition.

110 Understand your readers.

In Tips 1 through 5 you identified your readers in great detail. Make determinations based on their education level, position in the organization, knowledge of the topic, level of responsibility, age, biases, preferences, and attitudes. Understand how readers will internalize the information.

- Primary readers will act or make decisions based on the report.
- Secondary readers will be affected by the actions of the primary reader.
- Intermediate readers will be responsible for evaluating the report and making sure it reaches the right people.

111 Know what to include in an informal report.

An informal report is generally intended for a single reader or a small group of readers. It can range in length from a few paragraphs to a few pages. Because of their brevity, informal reports are customarily written in the form of letters, memos, or e-mail messages. Feasibility studies, investigative reports, progress reports, trip reports, seminar reports, and trouble reports all lend themselves to a casual format. Here's what to include in an informal report:

- Introduction or purpose
- Body
- Conclusions or recommendations.

(Check out Tip 13 for how to sequence information.)

Know what to include in a formal report.

A formal report is generally lengthy and is often the culmination of a project that may have taken a team of people weeks, months, or even years to complete. Formal reports can address issues as wide-ranging as new developments in a field, new product feasibility studies, services expansions, periodic reviews, and the like. (Check out Collaborative Writing, beginning on page 68.)

The term *formal* doesn't imply that the tone should be stuffy. It merely means that the report includes supplemental parts (as the following explains). You generally divide formal reports into three main parts (front matter, body, and back matter). Include any or all of the following sub-items in each part:

Front Matter

Precede the front matter with a letter of transmittal, which is basically a cover letter that identifies what you're sending and why you're sending it. Number the pages in the front matter with lowercase roman numerals. Front matter may include any or all of the following.

- **Title page:** Identifies the report, the completion date, the author, and the recipient.

- **Abstract:** Offers a condensed version of the report. (Check out Abstracts, beginning on page 49.)

- **Table of contents:** Lists all headings, subheads, and corresponding page numbers.

- **List of figures:** Lists all the figures in the report. (See the example that follows.)

- **List of tables:** Lists all the tables in the report. (See the example that follows.)

- **List of abbreviations and symbols:** Helps the reader who may not be familiar with abbreviations and symbols used. (See the example that follows.)

- **Preface or foreword (optional):** Announces the purpose, background, or scope. It may also acknowledge the people who participated in or helped with the project.

LIST OF FIGURES

LIST OF TABLES

LIST OF ABBREVIATIONS

ADP: Automatic Data Processing
AIS: Automated Information Systems
ANSI: American National Standards Institute

Body

This is the meat and potatoes of the report. Number the pages in the body with Arabic numerals. The body includes the following.

- **Executive summary:** Condenses the key issues in one or two pages. (Check out Executive Summaries, beginning on page 83.)

- **Introduction:** Indicates the intention of the report.

- **Conclusions, findings, or recommendations:** Answers the questions presented in the introduction.

Back Matter

The back matter is everything that comes after the body. Continue the Arabic numbering from the body. The back matter includes the following.

- **Bibliography:** Lists alphabetically all the written sources you consulted to prepare the report. (See the example that follows.)

- **Appendix:** Supplements the material in the body of the text (charts, tables, interview questions, and more). If you have more than one appendix, you may number the pages A-1, A-2, . . . B-1, B-2, etc.

- **Glossary:** Defines the terms in the report in alphabetical order. If you have a lot of technical terms, include a glossary.

- **Index:** Lists alphabetically all of the subjects in the report. Use your judgment as to whether or not you need an index. Be guided by content, not length. Ask yourself if you would want an index if you were in the reader's shoes.

BIBLIOGRAPHY

Creating America: A History of the United States, 1877 to the 21st Century. Evanston, Illinois: McDougal Littell Inc., 2003.

Boone, Louis E. *Quotable Business.* New York: Random House, 1992.

Lindsell-Roberts, Sheryl. *Loony Laws & Silly Statutes.* New York: Sterling Publishing, 1994.

Status reports are typically prepared by project teams to track and report a project's tasks, dates, delays, and completions. Status reports must be strategic, complete, and *useful*. The following *Before* example shows how one of my clients incorporated a list of program objectives into the status report sent each month to a branch of the military.

Before: Objectives are in a bulleted list.

> **Program Objectives**
> - Provide for Vertical Height Adjustment
> - Provide Rotated Equipment Installation
> - Design for Flexible Foundation
> - Design One Foundation for Each Unique Piece of Equipment
> - Use COTS When Possible

In the *After* status report, my client turned the bulleted list into a chart and included the task number and the status. The client also put this section at the front of each status report. This chart became the focal point of the report (rather than a ho-hum, repetitious section at the end), making it *useful* to the client and the project team. When anyone needed to see the continuity or current status of a task, it was right there up front.

After: Objectives are part of a chart.

Task No.	Program Objective	Status
1-A	Provide for Vertical Height Adjustment	Completed
2-B	Provide Rotated Equipment Installation	Completed
2-C	Design for Flexible Foundation	To be completed <date>
2-D	Design One Foundation for Each Unique Piece of Equipment	To be started <date>
3-A	Use COTS When Possible	Ongoing

SPEC SHEETS

*There is nothing so useless as doing efficiently
that which should not be done at all.*

PETER DRUCKER
American businessman and philosopher

A spec sheet (short for "specification sheet") describes work to be done. It ensures that all interested parties achieve the end result as effortlessly as possible. If you don't mention something explicitly, it may not get done. Spec sheets cover a wide variety of products and equipment, including software. Engineers, technicians, programmers, and other technical people may have occasions to write spec sheets. Everyone involved in developing a project will rely on the spec sheets for all the details of the project, much like everyone involved in constructing a building relies on the blueprints. Customers see only the end-user specs.

Understand how to develop specifications.

Engineers often design systems to meet a customer's requirements. The larger and more complicated the project is, the more important it is to create specs. Following is a four-step process for writing specs:

1. Get (from the customer) a statement of the problems and the requirements.

2. Analyze the problems and requirements and classify them.

3. Restate the requirements to the customer in your words to make sure you are on the same page.

4. Begin the writing process.

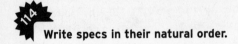

Write specs in their natural order.

You write specs in sequence because one builds upon the other. Spec sheets are always a work in progress and need to be updated as a project changes. If you relate this to building a house, the initial concept may be a rough sketch. The sketch evolves into a detailed drawing as the owner starts to think about heating and plumbing and other considerations. Following are guidelines for developing a spec sheet.

Phase	Type of Spec	Details
1	Requirement	When a company plans to introduce or update a product, it writes requirement specs to provide the design group with a starting point. These specs may be the outgrowth of a marketing analysis that studied the needs of the marketplace. At the very least, requirement specs include the following information.
		• **Definition of the application or product:** Detail all available information about the application or product.
		• **List of functions and capabilities:** Include information about what the application or product is capable of doing.
		• **Estimated cost of finished product:** Create a ballpark estimate of what the application or product should cost to make it competitive in the marketplace.
2	Functional	Functional specs expand on the list of capabilities iterated in the requirement specs. They deal with how the system operates. Here's some information to include in a functional spec:

- **System overview:** Explain the objectives, capabilities, methods, system operation, output, and what the system will and won't do.

- **Data dictionary:** Include all the facts and figures that enter the system or are produced by it. These include data names, abbreviations, data sources, ranges for numerical data, definitions or data descriptions, and codes and their meaning.

- **Input description:** Describe data that comes into the system and how the end user enters the data. This is key to the spec because the users are responsible for input; therefore, everything should be geared toward ease of use.

- **Operation description:** Explain what the system will do, under what conditions, and what will result.

- **Calculations:** Include formulas to determine how the system generates numbers for output.

- **File description:** Describe the purpose, content, use, and structure of the data files.

- **Other stuff:** Explain anything that's unique to the application or product.

3	*Design*	If you think functional specs are long, wait until you see the design specs. They add yet another level of detail and may include any or all of the following.

- **Relevant documents:** Include documents that have information relevant to the application or product. These are a critical resource to the technical writer who writes the manual.

- **Functional description:** Include a detailed description of the functionality. This description may be in the form of words or diagrams.

- **Interfaces:** Discuss interfaces to the product, including power requirements and anything else.

- **Programming considerations:** For software, deal with all aspects of the functionality the programmer works with.

- **Reliability:** Describe how reliable the product is and how often it should be serviced, maintained, or updated.

- **Diagnostic issues:** Describe the testing and evaluating required to ensure a quality product.

- **Deviations:** Describe changes that may be necessary as the project progresses.

---

4   *Test*

Before you bring hardware or software to market, you must test it under various conditions. Therefore, when you write test specs, you should include the following.

- **Relevant documents:** Include any documents that relate to similar hardware or software you've already developed that may be helpful to testers.

- **Product description:** Identify what is and isn't being tested.

- **Testing method:** Provide a step-by-step description of the testing procedure. This must also include the process for recording and reporting problems.

- **Precautions:** Identify any special care or issues that the tester must know. For example, you may want to document a secondary way to accomplish something (called a work-around) in the event the primary way doesn't work.

| 5 | *End user* | End-user specs are basically product-information sheets that ship with the product. They give users information about running the software or operating the equipment. End-user spec sheets may include features, strengths, weaknesses, product characteristics, support vendors, and more. |

*It usually takes me more than three weeks
to prepare a good impromptu speech.*

MARK TWAIN

When people think of speeches, they often think of politicians standing behind a podium. Some politicians, such as John Kennedy, Ronald Reagan, Bill Clinton, and others, are (or were) natural public speakers. And while it's true that some people are innately talented at public speaking, the good news is that anyone can write and deliver a successful speech that will be remembered for all the right reasons.

Public speaking doesn't have to be one of life's terrors. If you resist speaking before a group because you fear you'll drop dead from stage fright, you're not alone. Many people—even celebrated personalities such as Elvis Presley and Barbra Streisand—admit (or admitted) to suffering from stage fright. A little stage fright can even be positive, because the rush of adrenaline gives you energy.

Before you start writing a speech, be certain you've gone through the process in Part One. Also, check out PowerPoint Presentations, beginning on page 124, to learn how to prepare visual aids, if you need them.

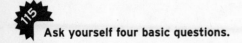

115
Ask yourself four basic questions.

Before you begin writing a speech, try this exercise. Write the answer to each of these questions in one sentence.

- **What's my topic?** If you're asked to speak at a professional conference on a process you developed, your topic may be obvious. However, if you're asked to speak at the Rotary Club, your topic isn't obvious. Discuss the topic with the person who asked you to speak.

Never put too many ideas or topics into your speech. Research shows that people remember very little from speeches, so give them one or two ideas to hang on to.

- **What's my message?** Check out Tip 7 to distill your key point into one sentence. If you can distill your key point into one sentence, then you can deliver a clear message to your audience.

- **What's my purpose?** Tip 6 talks about your purpose for writing (or in this case, speaking). Your purpose is what you want the audience to think, feel, or do.

- **What's in it for me?** Know your motivation. Are you tooting your own horn? Does this speech mean exposure and a boost to your career? Is it an opportunity to speak before a live audience? Any of these motivations are valid; just know what they are.

116
Make the opening and closing memorable.

People typically remember what you say first and what you say last. Don't waste either of these opportunities to make an impression. Limit your opening remarks to one or two minutes. The comedian George Jessel once said, "If you haven't struck oil in your first three minutes, stop boring."

- Relate a story.
- Ask a question.
- Use a quotation.

- Cite a statistic.
- Tell a joke.
- Show something.

Take one or two minutes to wrap up. A good speech ends with a bang. Recap your major theme or major points. End with an appeal. Use a quote. Relate a story. Ask a question.

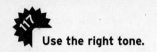

Use the right tone.

Use language that's clear, concise, and conversational. Keep the speech short and simple. Use positive words and the active voice. Be sensitive to word associations, sarcasm, and sexist language. For more information about using the right tone, check out Tips 21–28. Here are three specific ways to get the right tone and stress your message:

■ Phrase your sentences so they're strong and have impact.

> *Strong:* Financial planners believe that the market will continue to rise.
>
> *Weak:* There's a belief among financial planners that the market will continue to rise.

■ Use a highlighter or a bold font for text you want to emphasize. When speaking, use your voice to stress words or phrases.

> The goldfish is in the sink. (Nothing is stressed.)
> The **goldfish** is in the sink. (as opposed to the shark)
> The goldfish **is** in the sink. (in case you doubted it the first time)
> The goldfish is **in** the sink. (as opposed to near the sink)
> The goldfish is in the **sink**. (as opposed to in the bathtub)

■ Indicate pauses. Double slashes (//) may do the trick.

Check out the following opening statements made by Bill Clinton and Bob Dole at the first 1996 presidential debate. Notice the differences in tone and content. Do you think that speeches such as this one helped Bill Clinton to get elected?

President Bill Clinton's Opening Statement

Thank you, Jim. And thank you to the people of Hartford, our hosts. I want to begin by saying again how much I respect Senator Dole and his record of public service and how hard I will try to make this campaign and this debate one of ideas, not insults.

Four years ago I ran for president at a time of high unemployment and rising frustration. I wanted to turn this country around with a program of opportunity for all, responsibility from all, and an American community where everybody has a role to play. Four years ago you took me on faith. Now there's a record: Ten and a half million more jobs, rising incomes, falling crime rates and welfare roles, a strong America at peace.

We are better off than we were four years ago. Let's keep going. We cut the deficit by 60 percent. Now let's balance the budget and protect Medicare, Medicaid, education, and the environment. We cut taxes for 15 million working Americans. Now let's pass the tax cuts for education and child rearing, help with medical emergencies, and buying a home.

We passed family and medical leave. Now let's expand it so more people can succeed as parents and in the work force. We passed 100,000 police, the assault weapons ban, the Brady Bill. Now let's keep going by finishing the work of putting the police on the street and tackling juvenile gangs.

We passed welfare reform. Now let's move a million people from welfare to work. And most important, let's make education our highest priority so that every 8-year-old will be ready to read, every 12-year-old can log onto the Internet, every 18-year-old can go to college. We can build that bridge to the 21st century. And I look forward to discussing exactly . . .

Senator Bob Dole's Opening Statement

Thank you. Thank you, Mr. President, for those kind words. Thank the people of Hartford, the Commission, and all those out here who may be listening and watching. It's a great honor for me to be standing here as the Republican nominee. I'm very proud to be the Republican nominee reaching out to Democrats and Independents.

I have three very special people with me tonight: my wife, Elizabeth; my daughter, Robin, who has never let me down; and a fellow named Frank Carafa from New York, along with Ollie Manninen who helped me out in the mountains of Italy a few years back. I've learned from them that people do have tough times. And sometimes you can't go it alone.

And that's what America is all about. I remember getting my future back from doctors and nurses and a doctor in Chicago named Dr. Kalikian. And ever since that time, I've tried to give something back to my country, to the people who are watching us tonight. America is the greatest place on the face of the earth. Now, I know millions of you still have anxieties. You work harder and harder to make ends meet and put food on the table. You worry about the quality and the safety of your children, and the quality of education. But even more importantly, you worry about the future and will they have the same opportunities that you and I have had. And Jack Kemp and I want to share with you some ideas tonight.

Jack Kemp is my running mate, doing an outstanding job. Now, I'm a plain-speaking man and I learned long ago that your word was your bond. And I promise you tonight that I'll try to address your concerns and not try to exploit them. It's a tall order, but I've been running against the odds for a long time . . .

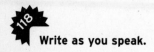

118

Write as you speak.

You write a speech to be heard, not read. The more conversational you can make it, the better you'll sound.

■ **Write short sentences.** Consider writing two simple sentences, rather than one long-winded sentence.

- **Use contractions.** Say *I'm* instead of *I am* or *can't* instead of *cannot.* They sound more conversational.

- **Write as you speak.** Winston Churchill proved that point in a comment against clumsy avoidance when he said, "This is the sort of English up with which I will not put."

- **Always read your speech aloud while you're writing it.** You'll know right away if you sound like a book or a real person talking!

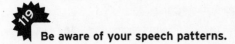

Be aware of your speech patterns.

After you write your speech, record it. (A tape recorder works well.) Listen to your recorded speech and pay attention to speech patterns that may distract the audience from what you're saying. For example, some speakers start with a low registration, work up to the emphasized words, then trail off. This pattern will generate major yawns. Other speakers interject "um" after every third word.

- **Use repetition for emphasis:** Repetition, used properly, gives strength to your statements.

  Strong: Why should we adopt this policy? We should adopt it because it will give us the competitive edge. And we should adopt it because it will give us a 50 percent profit.

  Weak: Why should we adopt this policy? Because it will give us the competitive edge and a 50 percent profit.

- **Include alliteration or rhymes:** These are often memorable parts of your talk.

  Alliteration: Really rigid requirements!

  Rhyme: You may remember the famous rhyme about the glove that came out of the O.J. Simpson trial: "If it doesn't fit, you must acquit."

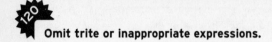

Omit trite or inappropriate expressions.

Following are inappropriate expressions that people often use. (The audience's possible interpretation is in parentheses.)

- "I'm really not prepared." *(Then why should we waste time listening to you?)*

- "I don't know why I was asked to speak here today." *(Are we being victimized by someone's poor judgment?)*

- "As unaccustomed as I am to . . ." *(Thanks for sharing that. I should have stayed away.)*

- "I won't take up too much of your time." *(This is going to be a sleeper.)*

- "I don't want to offend anyone, but . . ." *(Oh, here comes an insult.)*

- "Have you heard the one about . . ." *(Jerry Seinfeld he isn't.)*

- "Please give me a few more minutes." *(It's already been too long.)*

When you introduce a speaker, avoid the tiresome openers we all hear too often: "Ladies and gentlemen, this is a person who needs no introduction." "We're truly honored to have with us. . ." "Without further ado. . ." "It's indeed my privilege to introduce. . ." Consider a quick anecdote about the speaker or offer a few highlights of the speaker's career that make him worth listening to.

Think internationally.

It's a small world and shrinking quickly. International travel is commonplace. If you have occasion to speak before a foreign audience (including foreigners visiting or living in your country), display international savvy.

Consider these suggestions when speaking to people from other countries or cultures. The do's will entice your audience and the taboos will keep you from shooting yourself in both feet.

Do's

- Start your talk by expressing your sincere honor at being able to address the group.

- Be aware of current events that surround the country or culture and be sensitive to those issues.

- Quote a well-known person from your audience's country or culture. Make sure that person is someone your audience can admire.

- Bolster the need for international communication. Use statistics, anecdotes, or stories.

- Deliver a powerful line or phrase in the audience's native language and be aware of how things translate.

President John F. Kennedy delivered a speech in Germany during his presidency. He gave a very emphatic hand gesture and bellowed out, "Ich bin ein Berliner!" His German audience cheered as he uttered these words. However, Kennedy was later criticized for the lack of knowledge of German grammar displayed in this phrase. It is more usual to say "Ich bin Berliner" (without the indefinite article *ein*) to mean "I am a Berliner." The phrase *Ich bin ein Berliner* invites the interpretation "I am a jelly doughnut."

Taboos

- Never (inadvertently) offend your audience with offhand generalizations. For example, if you're from the US and speaking to people from Greece, don't announce, "In the US all the diners are owned by Greeks." How would you feel if you were traveling abroad and heard someone say, "All Americans talk loudly and expect you to understand English"?

- Never tell off-color jokes or use profanities. That holds true no matter who's in the audience.

- Avoid idiomatic expressions that may not be understood.

Blogs—the abbreviated term for weblogs—appear to visitors as Web pages. At first, blogs were just cool. They were used as online diaries or journals. However, blogs are no longer merely teenage ruminations on life. Blogging has grown into a completely new way of doing business. Blogs can be used to share thoughts, ideas, build personal and corporate credibility, and grab search-engine attention.

Posting your blog

In recent times there has been a revolution in the way we can send messages—through e-mails, Web pages, text messages, and blogs. But the same rules of the road apply to this sort of writing as to others.

- Contribute only something of value.
- Use descriptive headlines.
- Keep paragraphs short and to the point.
- Write as you speak (that is, conversationally).
- Divide information into specific categories.
- Post frequently.
- Use lots of links; they're free.
- Don't over-engineer and brand-bloat the blog.
- Don't get involved in flame wars when people post negative comments.
- Appreciate the good comments and feedback, and respond to them.

Posting to someone else's blog

Remember that each blog you visit is someone's Internet home. You wouldn't enter someone's home and insult the host. The same holds true for blogging.

- Don't get personal.
- Don't be a spoiler by divulging information such as the ending to a hot new book or new movie.
- Stay on topic.
- Keep comments short and to the point.

> *There is no reason anyone would want*
> *a computer in their home.*

KEN OLSEN
former chairman and founder of
Digital Equipment Corporation

The Web with its tangle of competing sites is like Times Square with its multitude of billboards vying for attention. You want your site to be visited, and visited repeatedly—much like a bookstore that becomes a haunt because customers find the atmosphere inviting and conducive to browsing. Make your website rich in content and functionality and you will motivate your visitors to keep coming back.

Successful websites cater to the needs of the visitor: card companies automatically send electronic birthday cards to your friends and relatives; shipping services offer online tracking and delivery confirmation; banks let you access account information and pay bills online.

Think of what you can offer to make your website one that people visit regularly and recommend to others. Here are some suggestions: Hot industry trends. News releases. Specials. Newsletters. Contests. Online customer service. Surveys. Expert answers. Weblogs. Meeting boards. Links to timely articles. Weekly or monthly tips. Order checking capability.

 Before you start writing your Web text, be certain you've gone through the process in Part One.

Note: People who visit your website are called *visitors*. Therefore, in this section you see the term *visitors* rather than *readers*.

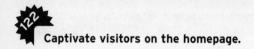

Captivate visitors on the homepage.

Think of the Web as a giant magazine rack and the viewer as someone scanning the front covers of all the magazines. Within a few seconds the viewer will decide to stay or look elsewhere. Catch the visitor's attention immediately, or he's back on his horse galloping to another site. The most important thing you can give your homepage is valuable content.

- Reflect the personality of your company with the text and graphics.
- Keep the homepage simple and orderly.
- Make the homepage (and all pages) easy to skim. (People don't read Web pages; they skim them.)
- Write in an objective style, rather than in a promotional style.
- Keep the homepage short and to the point.
- Use the homepage to offer information, not just a sales pitch.
- Minimize scrolling.
- Create navigation that's easy to understand and simple to use.

Highlight what differentiates you from your competitors.

Competition is part of business. In addition to delivering what your customers want, you need to know what the competition is doing and how you're doing it better, how you're more cost-effective, or how you perform your job differently. It's not enough to say that you have "excellent customer services" or "superior products." Everyone says that. *Think outside the box!*

The number of competitors you face online grows daily. Ask yourself, Why should my viewers do business with me? You must be able to answer that, or it's only a matter of time before you go out of business.

- Understand what your customers want, and what your competitors don't offer.

- Know the strengths and weaknesses of the competitors in your industry.
- Become familiar with the product lines they offer.
- Identify what makes each company competitive.

> Look at the websites of your competitors to see how they tantalize or frustrate visitors.

124
Identify key words and phrases so readers find your site easily.

"Build it and they will come" doesn't apply to websites. What good is a dynamic website if people don't find it? Target your writing for search-engine optimization. There are many resources to help you do this, and your Web guru is the best resource. Once you identify the key words and phrases, pepper your site with them. This will increase your chances of being found by the search engines.

> As a business writer, here are a few search words I use on my website:
>
> - business writing
> - business communications
> - marketing communications
> - technical writing.
>
> I left out *marcom* or *marcomm* (often used as an abbreviation for "marketing communications") because there are several companies by that name, and I don't want to point to the competition.

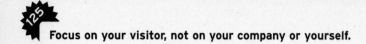

Focus on your visitor, not on your company or yourself.

Viewers aren't interested in you; they're interested in themselves and how your business can benefit them. If your site is all about you, visitors will look elsewhere. You don't want to be like the opera singer who warms up with *me, me, me, me.*

> I recently visited a client—an architectural firm. Posted on the bulletin board was the copy of a cover letter that accompanied a proposal my client had requested. My client drew a circle around each mention of the writer (*me, my, our*) and a square around each mention of the client (*you, your*). The letter had 28 circles and 3 squares. My client sent the proposal back with the notation "28 to 3. You lose!" Although this example doesn't relate to websites per se, it does point out that no one wants to read about you.

Stress benefits, not features.

This comes right out of Sales 101. Tell your visitors what's in it for them in terms of benefits. Don't drone on about your state-of-the-art facility and your detailed manufacturing process. Your customers buy benefits, not features. A feature is an attribute of a product or service. A benefit is an advantage of using a product or service. Benefits appeal to a person's emotional or practical needs. Increased revenue, a more stylish look, a better quality of life, a decrease in production time of 20 percent, reduced assembly time, or a higher yield are examples of benefits.

Benefits and features of an electric drill

Benefits	Features
• Makes clean, deep holes	• Made of titanium
• Drills holes in seconds	• Is UL-approved
• Is lightweight	

Benefits and features of lipstick

Benefits	Features
• Makes you look more attractive	• Made with tetroberinbum (made up)
• Stays on for 12 hours	• Comes with aluminum case
• Doesn't smear	

127

Craft compelling, informational headlines.

Make your headlines serve as ads for the copy that follows. (Check out Tip 12 for a full discussion of headlines.) Studies show that only one in five people read beyond the headlines. The right wording in your headline increases the sales conversion rate by 1700 percent. Here are some suggestions for writing headlines:

- Include the single most important benefit you offer; for example, you might begin with "Always on time, on budget."
- Mention your target visitor in the headline. For example, if you target dentists, use *dentists* in your headline.
- Include *you* and *your*.
- Use power words such as *discover, now, sale, breakthrough*—words that grab attention.

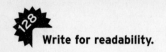

Write for readability.

Readability is a measure of how easily your writing is read and understood. By maximizing the readability of your website, you help visitors understand what you say quickly and clearly. Web visitors want information instantly, so it's critical that key points stand out. Here are some tips for creating a readable website:

Formatting

- Always start with a compelling headline. Visitors read headlines if nothing else.
- Use lots of subheads.
- Include bold text sparingly. Bold works well for headlines. Don't, however, scatter boldface in the text, because it can be confusing or distracting.
- Include bullets, numbers, graphs, and tables to convey critical information.
- Use the inverted pyramid (borrowed from the news industry). List key information first, followed by supporting details.
- Sequence for emphasis. You capture visitors with the opening and closing.
- Limit each page to 100–250 words. Less is more!

Text

- Divide the text into manageable chunks of information.
- Use short, high-impact sentences.
- Use the active voice.
- Avoid internal jargon and language.
- Include quotes and testimonials, when appropriate.
- Cut anything that doesn't add value to the visitor.

Design

- Avoid horizontal lines, which may be seen as a barrier and stop the reader from scrolling.

- Consider vertical lines to indicate there's more to see.
- Keep headlines close to the text they describe.
- Write headlines in upper- and lowercase characters, which are easier to read onscreen than all caps.
- When generating tables, remember that people typically scan down columns, not across.
- Choose a type and background in colors of high contrast. Black type on a white background is the most readable.

Go modular. Think about the content and how the average person will access your pages. Keep the topic and content of each page focused on one complete thought or idea. This means each page should stand alone, if possible. People have different browsing styles, so they will view your website from different paths. Consider having the same information in several places.

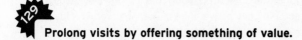

Prolong visits by offering something of value.

Offer an e-book, provide online registration, include a chatroom, add frequently asked questions (FAQs), provide links to cool sites, and more.

Don't include your mission statement on your website. A mission statement is of no value to your visitors. They don't care about your company's goals or objectives; they care about what you can do for them.

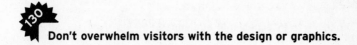

Don't overwhelm visitors with the design or graphics.

Contrary to popular belief, viewers' eyes aren't drawn to dazzling graphics in multitudes of colors. Viewers value substance over glitz. Here are some suggestions for using graphics appropriately:

- Choose your text and background colors carefully. Dark text on a light background is easier to read than light text on a dark background.
- Design your illustrations so they attract your visitor's attention, not distract from the content.

 White space (space between elements) takes on added importance on the Web because more strain is placed on the eyes than with print material. Treat white space as more than just a background. Treat it as an integral part of your design, and you will increase the power of your message.

 On the Web, audio is powerful. It's commonly known that the more senses you engage, the greater the chance of enticing people. Visitors respond to audio in a way they don't respond to words alone, no matter how great your copy is. Don't hit people with audio as soon as they arrive at your site, however. Provide a click so visitors can hear the following:

- Your voice, to remove some of the anonymity of the Web experience
- Testimonials from clients/customers that make you very credible
- Playback of seminars or teleconferences so visitors can capture information they may have missed (they may promote you by passing this along to others)
- Tips that give short pieces of information quickly
- Instructions to people who don't like to read.

131

Be sensitive to international audiences.

As Internet access grows across the globe, so do translation and download problems. The following are some guidelines to help you meet the needs of worldwide viewers:

- **Work with a translator.** If the site is to be translated, identify the languages. Send text, menus, and entries to the translator to learn of potential problems.

- **Be aware of download time.** There are many parts of the world that have slow modems and Internet access that bills by the minute. Users in these regions (and many are right here in the United States) will visit sites that are quick to download.

- **Create sites that are printable.** In parts of the world where Internet access is very expensive, viewers often share computers. They tend to print out websites and distribute hard-copy pages.

Understand why websites don't bring in new business.

There are a number of reasons websites aren't successful. Here are a few:

- **Lack of keywords.** You must have the keywords your audience will use to search for your site. Otherwise, people won't know you're there. These words must be peppered throughout the site because you don't know where people enter.

- **Bleeding-edge technology.** Don't use the latest technology with all the bells and whistles just because you can. That's akin to generating documents that look like circus posters just because you have a word processor. Include only what you need.

- **Sensory overload.** Don't use images that have an overpowering effect on the human peripheral vision.

- **Hard-to-read colors.** There are still websites that have black backgrounds with yellow lettering, or something equally awful. Use appropriate, readable colors.

- **Outdated information.** Keep your site current. You need a gardener to weed your Web garden and plant new flowers. An outdated site is the sign of an outdated company.

- **Long downloads.** Human factors guidelines show that if a file takes longer than eight seconds to download, visitors lose interest. People still use dial-up modems, and download time may be a significant factor.

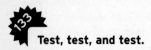

133

Test, test, and test.

Following are some ways to make sure your website is ready for prime time:

- Test on different browsers.
- Test on Macs and PCs.
- Test on a variety of monitors.
- Make sure your links work and go to where they should.
- Be sure download time is quick.
- Ask people you trust for their opinions.

Many things that make the Web so nifty (audio, animation, streaming videos, colorful graphics, and more) are barriers to people with disabilities.

- Steer clear of design elements that aren't compatible with text-only browsers and adaptive technologies.

- Include text equivalents for audio elements and graphics.

- Design for people who are colorblind by creating text and graphics that are independent of color.

- Provide HTML versions where possible.

Check out http://webxact.watchfire.com, a free online service that lets you check your site for quality, accessibility, and privacy.

*Words are, of course, the most powerful drug
used by mankind.*

RUDYARD KIPLING

The term *white paper* comes from the term *white book*, which refers to an official publication of a national government. A white paper may be a government document or other authoritative report. A commercial white paper describes a product, service, or technology. It is a low-cost way for you to promote your product and gain an advantage over your competitors. Unlike articles, which may reflect the writer's point of view, white papers aim to give unbiased information.

Before you start writing your white paper, be certain you've gone through the process in Part One.

Use a logical structure.

Consider the following structure in a white paper:

- **Introduction.** Cover the high-level issues and include recommendations or conclusions.

- **High-level solution.** Include tables, graphs, or charts to support your argument and provide a contrast to the main text.

- **Solution details.** Explain how the service, business model, or technology works. This is the core of your white paper.

- **Business benefits.** Include return on investment (ROI), customer quotes, and anything that highlights the value of your topic. Don't take this section for granted—not all your competitors will be able to supply such endorsements.

- **Summary.** As with an article, write the summary as if it were a standalone document. Many readers will skip the rest of the document and read only the summary.

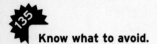

Know what to avoid.

People who read white papers typically want in-depth, detailed information that addresses how a product or service solves a specific problem. When white papers aren't successful, it's often because they're written by nerdy types and the text is difficult to digest. Here are some things to avoid:

- Technical acronyms
- Difficult terminology
- Technical complexity.

ABOUT THE AUTHOR

 Sheryl wears a lot of hats, just as you do. First and foremost, she's married to Jon, her best friend and life partner, and is the mother of Marc and Eric, who continue to inspire her as they live their lives with open minds and hearts. Sheryl's grandchildren, Brooke, Jill, and Brian, complete her life with a sense of perspective and immeasurable joy.

For more than twenty years Sheryl has been the Principal of Sheryl Lindsell-Roberts & Associates, a business writing and marketing communications firm. Sheryl's team has helped companies to increase revenue through strategic business writing. They have generated proposals, brochures, and websites that have helped companies to close multimillion-dollar contracts. This book is the outgrowth of all her professional experience.

Sheryl feels fortunate to have a job that would be her hobby if it weren't her profession. Between writing and delivering business-writing and technical-writing workshops, she has written nineteen other books for the professional and humor markets. Some of her hot sellers are *Strategic Business Letters and E-mail* and *Mastering Computer Typing*, published by Houghton Mifflin; *Technical Writing for Dummies*, published by John Wiley; and *Loony Laws & Silly Statutes*, published by Sterling Publishing.

When her life gets more complicated than it needs to be, Sheryl's warm-weather nirvana is her thirty-foot sailboat, *Worth th' Wait*. She and her husband Jon are aboard every weekend the temperature rises above sixty and the seas aren't too treacherous. (They've also been out there when they were too treacherous, but not by choice.) She doesn't bring a suitcase stuffed with clothes because there isn't room to put too much; she's learned to minimize. All she needs is sunscreen, a few pairs of shorts, some T-shirts, a good book, and Elvis tapes. Sheryl believes that everyone needs a nirvana—a time when the past and future are cut off and only the present exists—even if it's a spot under a tree or the corner of a room.

When she's not writing or sailing, Sheryl travels, paints (watercolors and oils, not walls), gardens, photographs nature, reads, skis, eats strawberry cheesecake, and works out at the gym (she says that after the cheesecake she needs the gym). She tries to live each day to the fullest! For more information, please check out www.sherylwrites.com.

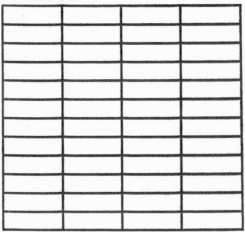